The Most Loved

A Love... A Story... A Life

The Most Loved

A Love... A Story... A Life

by Leandrea Rivers

Written and Published by: Leandrea Rivers
lea@leabiz.com | www.TheMostLovedBook.org
Facebook: The Most Loved A Love A Story A Life

ISBN: 978-0-615-81045-4

First Edition 2013

Category: Motivational / Inspirational / Empowerment

Library of Congress Cataloging-in-Publication Data

Edited by: Emily Rogers

Photography (front cover) by: Rassi Dennard

Photography (back cover) by: Mike n Me Photography

Cover Design and Book Formatting-Layout by:
Eli Blyden | www.CrunchTimeGraphics.NET

Printed in the United States of America

Preface

"The Most Loved" A Love, A Story, A Life is based on a true story. This book is written with the intent that readers will gain an entirely new perspective on life— guaranteed! Society's "preconceived notions" regarding the definition of healthy relationships will be redefined. Healing, restoration, forgiveness; the exchanging of thoughts, our communication and how we behave in relationships, will all become more vivid through one woman's bravery and transparency as her life unfolds.

This book serves to inspire those who carry excess baggage (lack of trust, insecurities, infidelity, domestic abuse, spiritual warfare, post-traumatic stress disorder (PTSD), etc.). Readers will be able to identify themselves, a friend, or a loved one throughout this book. Where does the healing begin? Where does the accountability begin? Where "in space and time" will one truly forgive "self" and others? Lastly, when will that "ah ha" moment come? Is it when one realizes that their excess baggage has cost them the only person they ever truly loved? When will one forget and move on from the past, the haunted chapters, start over in life as a new, whole individual? These are some of the questions readers will find themselves answering ....

Table of Contents

Preface v

Introduction 1

1
Rest In Peace 3

2
Hush, Don't You Cry 9

3
Summer Rains 19

4
Daddy's Baby Girl 31

5
A Faded Mirror 35

6
My Joy 47

7
A Time to Forgive 53

8
A Different Me 67

9
Forsake Thee Not 89

10
Amazing Graces...................................... 101

11
Forgive Us Father 115

12
Fools Rush In... 117

13
The Glamorous Life.................................. 121

14
Guess Who's For Dinner?.......................... 131

15
You Lost A Good Thing 135

16
First Impressions..................................... 147

17
House Warming 157

18
Beach Bums 165

19
The Air I Breathe 173

20
Indecent Exposure................................... 185

21
Killing Me Softly 193

22
Countdown ... 9, 8, 7................................ 203

23
It's A Long Road 211

24
Open Up 217

25
Bone Deep... 225

26
Mirror, Mirror 229

27
New York, New York 237

28
Who Is He? 239

29
Pampering Anyone?... 243

30
Someone Call 911 247

31
Surprise, Surprise.. 251

32
Hurt So Bad... 257

33
Just Fine 261

34
Locked Up... 267

35
King and Queen 269

36
Blood Is Thick 275

37
City Of Dreams 279

38
A Bond Not Easily Broken 289

39
You Have The Rights 297

40
Our Love 301

41
Dead at My Brother's Hands 303

42
Hear My Plea 309

43
Seeds To Bear 313

Acknowledgements 319

Introduction

"*People, they think I have this life that some only dream about. If only they can live my life for a day; I promise they'd give it back! When trouble comes my way, to the water is where I escape… it's a place of intimacy… it's where God and I meet. It's my refuge. It's my peace. It's my tranquility.*"

Summer Covington, a love child; she had eyes that could pierce any soul with love, a smile that was infectious upon sight, and skin that had been passionately stroked by Florida's sun rays. You name it and she had come across it all … *"You can get whatever you want from a man Summer, you have everything it takes, use it!"* She was told time and time again.

Her eyes had not seen, her ears had not heard, yet "she" had been promised the entire world. *"Summer you are this, Summer you are that! Summer, I'll do this and Summer, I'll do that."* She had been flattered and "lied to" to death by everyone; friends, family, lovers, even the strangers who, in that split second brushed up against her in elevators, in malls, and in office hallways.

Failure and defeat was something no one was willing to accept from Summer—and I do mean no one! Many saw in her what Summer couldn't see in herself. Numerous people in her life would stop at nothing to belittle, lie, steal and cheat; destroying her self-esteem, reputation, lifestyle and eventually her family!

Enter inside a world seen through the eyes of a forgiving spirit, a strong-willed and determined lady; a lady willing to win no matter how many bruised falls or romantic relationships she found herself in while "searching for love in all the wrong places." Summer's amazing faith continually pushed her forward, regardless of the countless times her physical strength failed her. Summer continuously crawled through life's tunnels and found God's magnificent rays of light awaiting her!

1

Rest In Peace

*D*eeper and deeper I submerged into the darkness, oblivious to what had actually happened to cause me to feel as though I was drowning. Why had I suddenly started sinking so fast? No life jacket, vest, or flotation device … nothing!

The voice inside my head said, *Do something! Fight Summer, fight!* That was all I heard within me. So, I did as any good little girl would, I obeyed and I fought! I began to quickly kick and push with both arms spread out above my head—an attempt to force the weight of my body upwards. Chlorine stung my eyes as tears ran down my face. I pushed deeper and deeper into the water, finally forcing it to give way to my tiny feet.

I heard angry screams coming from a woman's voice. Although not quite clear, it sounded like my mommy's voice, "Lex are you crazy? You go get my baby now!" she yelled. Before I knew it, I had "doggie paddled" my way up towards the light. Gasping for air and coughing up water, I fought for dear life all the way to the top. There was hope! I was finally safe again.

At three years old, I couldn't comprehend what my daddy had done, and who knows, maybe he was too intoxicated with beer to understand himself. But, everything he did that day had prepared me for this dreadful day; a day that I wasn't quite ready to face.

"The best gift you can ever give to your child as a parent is to lead them to Christ," I said. My voice began to crack before the crowd of mourners in the church.

"My daddy gave me that. He knew there would be moments like this when he wouldn't be able to be here for me, but God would always be there!" I told them.

The time had finally arrived to lay Lex Covington to rest and a proper, honorable, military burial was what Lex had earned the right to.

The United States flag draped my daddy's blue coffin. The infantry regiment's honor guards were already in place, and ready to pay their respect to the deceased soldier's next of kin. My daddy was committed to his *duty;* he had served with honor, and he always remained faithful to his country.

With each fired rifle, I shook, fighting back the tears. Large, black "Hollywood" shades covered my face to hide my emotions from the crowd. As each shell casing fell to the ground, I continued to shake inside; I was reliving the days before in my head. I felt empty and completely numb, but I knew that I had to remain strong for my two younger brothers, Nick and Jay.

The flag presentation was impressive. It exemplified discipline, obedience, and confidence found in only true soldiers. I sat there feeling proud that my daddy had served his country, but at the same time, I felt cheated, even robbed! Serving his country is what ultimately led us there to his demise.

At some point during the burial service, my mind drifted off into space. The days leading up to that very moment all played back before me so vividly. Day by day, hour by hour, and minute by minute, the days replayed themselves like the large hands of a grandfather clock; going around and around in a circle through my head.

Ring, ring. "Hello?" I whispered. I was always careful not to disturb my coworkers when my personal phone rang when I was at work.

"Summer, your daddy is gone baby," my aunt's voice was faint as it echoed through my ear piece.

"Gone, what do you mean gone?" I tried to comprehend what she meant exactly by the word "gone."

"Baby, he is no longer with us," said Aunt Nat.

This must be some sick joke or perhaps, some horrific mistake of some sort. I thought, as I tried desperately to rationalize the tragic news. I felt as though my heart had sprung right out of my chest cavity and fell onto the floor before me and exploded. Then, it hit me, hard. It felt like I had run into a piece of metal ... my daddy was gone! He was dead!

"No, No, No!" I cried out uncontrollably. My moans must have been bone shivering to the innocent bystanders, now surrounding me. It was far too much pain for me to bear alone; others must have felt it too ....

My head fell into my lap from the weight of heaviness. *I'm not prepared nor ready to receive this type of news.* I thought. My anguish must have been felt throughout the entire office. Managers ran to me from various departments in an attempt to comfort and aide me.

My face was covered in tears. My body was weak and limp. I sat there unable to move. My body had become demobilized. My head felt too heavy to lift.

"Summer, lift your head sweetie," I heard a voice say.

I couldn't, I simply couldn't! I tried. I tried with every fiber of being within me, but I was frozen. My mobility skills were somehow detached and were not cooperating with my brain cells at all. I had never, ever, felt such an ache; I was shaken to my core at that moment. The room had instantly become a pit of darkness.

I felt like the same lost, frightened and scared little girl, just as I had so many years ago, the day my daddy tossed me into the swimming pool to save myself.

Strange arms embraced me. "Summer, what's wrong sweetie?" I heard voices echoing behind me.

"No! No! No!" Escaped from my mouth and there was nothing, absolutely nothing I could do to control my words.

I was hopeless. I was lost. I was confused. To sum it all up, I was simply distraught. I cried uncontrollably until I was too weak to cry any longer.

"Summer, we need to get you some fresh air to help you breathe sweetie," my manager, Brittany said. She and another manager, Carolyn, slowly lifted me up from my chair to my feet.

"My daddy is dead," I muttered as an explanation for my state of being.

No sir, not all of my memories of my daddy were fond ones, and my childhood certainly was far from a bed of red roses, but *everyone has a story, even if every story is never told!*

The Most Loved

2

Hush, Don't You Cry

"No, stop it … don't put your hands on me!" I could hear my mommy's cries and screams from the couch in the family room. I wanted to cover my ears, but at the same time I was too afraid I wouldn't be able to hear my mommy anymore. I was so terrified for her. I would just sit on the couch crying and shaking with nervousness, and biting my nails until they were sore.

A child, so young, I couldn't wrap my little brain around any of the domestic abuse which took place. I just remembered my mommy's lip always being red, swollen, and her face being red, black and blue.

I couldn't recall seeing too many other black women who had her features. She was exotic. Especially her eyes, they were alluring. She was always so pretty, so well dressed and nice to everyone. *Why would my daddy want to beat her?* I questioned.

I was a petite toddler, but my mind was so very big! Having extremely bright and intelligent parents, I didn't have any say in whether or not I would be *above average*.

At three years old, how could my mind have consumed all that I witnessed? Although buried deep, I could pull back layer after layer; I could dig up our family dirt at any given moment and recall the events so vividly.

Why was everyone in the house getting struck and beaten? Everyone—except me. Confused, I simply wondered when I heard the frequent thumps against the walls.

Some called me the *Love Child*. I was the only child they conceived together prior to my parent's short marriage. My mommy had a son before me, Kurtis. We called him "Kurt" for short. Kurtis had a "dark chocolate" complexion and very slanted eyes, like almonds, and he also had a slender build. He had the most beautiful, bright, white smile that you would ever lay eyes on. Unfortunately, Lex never accepted him.

"Summer, you could never do any wrong in your daddy's eyes," said my Aunt Vanessa. I remember she would stare at me with those hazel eyes of hers as though it was my fault. I was just a little girl. I wish I could have changed my daddy ways, but I couldn't. I hated what he did to my mommy and my older brother; yet still, I loved him with all of my heart. Although I was young, maybe inside I knew he was mentally sick ... that something was wrong with him internally.

My brother's biological father, Tony, lived in the same city as us and was raising his other children. Who would have ever thought, with a child living so close to him, that a father could allow another man to abuse his son? The truth of the matter, he never had anything to do with Kurtis because of his ignorant, new wife.

She was too insecure to accept the fact that my brother Kurtis came along long before she was ever in the picture. Her lack of confidence in herself, and lack of trust in her husband, and/or perhaps, the fact that my mother was very beautiful, may have caused too much fear in her. Perhaps, my mother and Kurtis were both a threat to her marriage, in her own insecure mind.

My mommy didn't give a *flying hoot* about Kurtis' weak ass dad, Tony. She was too busy trying to keep all of us alive and safe.

Despite all of the mental and physical abuse, my mommy tried with everything in her to make their marriage work. She hoped and prayed that Lex would change. She didn't want to someday end up killing him to prevent him from killing her.

Perhaps, Tony was oblivious as to what was really going on. Had Tony been present from the very start, maybe, just maybe, none of this would have ever taken place. Who really was to blame?

Fact remained, Tony was an absentee parent and no parent should be excused from the parenting equation. Kurt's abuse lied upon all of their hands; Charlie's, Lex's, and Tony's. Whether or not my mommy was trying to make her marriage work, staying in a domestic violence situation was not helping us as children. The real damage was sure to follow years later for Kurtis and me.

Often, I wanted to grab my mommy and brother and just hug them. I heard the belt buckle and the lashes hitting my brother as he sucked in his cries; most times in an attempt to spare me from despair as I cried out for him. Other times he couldn't help but cry out for help; crying for someone to save him from those undeserved beatings and torture.

"Hands along your side and keep your head straight ahead boy," he would say to my brother as he marched him into the garage. He did this as if he was the "sergeant" and my brother was the "private."

My brother always obeyed in silence; never being disobedient. Even in the midst of his abuse he remained respectful. My daddy was careful to never allow me to see the actual beatings.

So many times I wanted to grab my daddy's hand; I imagined myself telling him *"Stop it! Stop it daddy, stop hitting my big brother!"* Maybe that's exactly what it would have taken for my daddy to snap out of it and see how he was destroying us all. Looking back, it all makes sense to me now why my older brother was always so excessively protective of me.

My daddy's behavior, was it something that my daddy had witnessed as a child also? Or better yet, was he also abused at the hands of his own father? Was it perhaps, his years in the Vietnam War that had tarnished his mind and brought about the violence? *Why, why, why was my daddy doing this to his own family?*

Regardless, nothing could take away the joy Kurtis had in his heart. I admired him for that.

We were inseparable. We had so much love in our hearts for each other. Kurtis and I had seen and been through so much together to be so very young.

Kurtis could have resented me, but instead he chose to love me all the more. I'm sure in Kurt's heart and mind he vowed to never let anyone hurt me as he had been hurt time and time again.

On the surface, I smiled. Kurt smiled—we all smiled. No one would ever truly know how much we were hurting behind closed doors. Well, yeah … they knew! My mommy's family knew. Lex's family knew. Friends knew. Neighbors in our cul-de-sac knew. Everyone knew, but no one would stand up to Lex. No one, except for my crazy ass granddaddy Charlie.

My mommy was named after my Granddaddy Charlie. He wanted his first born to be a boy. Well, "Charlie" came out to be a girl. Of course, they couldn't resist letting a good wholesome name like 'Charlie' go to waste. So guess who was privileged to be named after granddaddy? Yep, you guessed it ... my mommy, *Charlie*. The honor was all hers.

As any proud daughter would be, my mommy was indeed, proud to have her dad's name. With her good looks and personality, no one really cared what her name was. Most times people just called her "Beautiful" anyways.

Everyone in our tight knit, cul-de-sac neighborhood knew of my daddy's hot temper and jealous ways towards my mommy. Many brushed it off due to our home being the social spot for our relatives, close family friends and neighbors. Lex's charm often times, would quickly erase what was transpiring behind closed doors.

Our swimming pool was the size of a community center's pool; it was enormous. There were concrete brick walls surrounding the backyard of our property, that even the tallest man would have difficulty climbing over. We were living in a fortress and my daddy was king.

My parents had all of the finer things in life; a new car, a nice home, nice clothes, well-mannered children. My daddy had everything one needed to entertain for a weekend, or even a week. Many times it seemed as though friends and relatives never wanted to leave and would always find reasons to stay beyond their scheduled visits.

With a large pool table in the three car garage, the garage was the man cave of the house. The men would drink beer, shoot pool and there was always plenty of trash-talking to go along with all of their fun.

"Lex hand me another beer man," my daddy's best friend Ted said smiling. Ted was "Uncle Teddy" to me. He and my daddy had been buddies since college.

My daddy would always sneak and give me beer. My mommy hadn't a clue that I was getting wasted. I would gulp the beer down as though I had a hole in my throat (probably why I can't stand the taste of beer to this day).

"Hold on, hold on baby girl," my daddy said.

"Man, Summer drinking that beer like it was baby milk," my Uncle Ted said as he laughed.

Imagine an adorable little three year old girl with thick, curly hair and a pony tail on the top of her head, gut sticking from beneath her halter top, tagging alongside her daddy's every move. Well, that was me, Summer.

Whatever my daddy did, I would look up wanting to try also. My beer gut was my sworn initiation as one of his "partners in crime male club." I witnessed the cursing each other out while his friends played their card table games. Granted, I was never foolish enough to ever repeat the swearing, I knew better than that!

My daddy could pull the wool over anyone's eyes. Mommy was unfortunately the one who fell hopelessly in love with him. Why marry someone so beautiful and become so fearful of someone else taking them away? If he couldn't have handled it, he should have stayed in his own lane.

Maybe it was the fact that Lex knew he loved women and was capable of doing things he probably shouldn't have done as a married man. You know, the person accusing all of the time is typically the one guilty of the crime. *Hmmm ....*

I'm sure Lex thought if he could do it while claiming to love her, that she could do it to him too. That was straight foolishness though. My mommy would never have cheated on my daddy, ever! She was in love with him in spite of his control issues. He was simply trying to justify his own decisions.

The makeup could only cover up so much before I remember my granddaddy coming over to our home to confront Lex. My mommy packed us up, left my daddy, and then, we returned right back home to my daddy. This went on many, many times; us leaving and later returning.

One day, my mommy got wind of my daddy abusing Kurtis. She had no clue what had been transpiring. Often times, the abuse occurred after she left for work. Once this source of news came to the forefront, there was no way she could remain. She loved us kids more than she loved Lex. She had to leave!

She left the house behind, the prestige, and the status; everything, except Kurtis and me. She had finally built up enough courage to leave Lex.

The Most Loved

3

Summer Rains

eing a single parent now meant longer hours; especially, during hurricane seasons here in Florida. Considering the nature of my mommy's job as a 911 operator; it was mandatory that she worked during bad storm seasons. Our livelihood now depended on hurricanes, rain and lightning storms. The overtime granted to her was a great help; enough to afford Kurtis and I the same lifestyle we had grown accustomed to living before she left Lex.

My Aunt Stefani and Uncle Damien would often take up the slack for my mommy's absences. Uncle Damien was a beast. He had big legs, big arms, and a big head. His thick football player neck topped it all off. He was simply a big guy! Damien was a big, red guy with freckles. He was a football player.

Both he and my Aunt Stefani were very active in sports. Damien was a football captain and Stefani was on the cheerleading squad. Aunt Stefani had such a cute figure that all of the boys were crazy about. But, Stefani wasn't falling for the lame game—she was hard on the fellas.

My Grandma Carolyn made sure that they both were raised in the church. Neither my Uncle Damien nor my Aunt Stefani were going to bring any foolishness up in Grandma's house. We spent many weekends over there while mommy worked. Even though they were our aunt and uncle, we were more like brothers and sisters.

Somehow, I was always the target of pranks. It probably had something to do with me always ratting them out to Grandma.

"Summer, we are going to time you to see how fast you can run," Kurtis said. All of them laughed, I should have known they were up to no good.

"One, two, three," Uncle Damien counted.

"Summer, go faster," Aunt Stefani chimed in. I ran as fast as I could. As soon as they saw me turn the corner into the dining room, Kurtis stuck out his leg and down I came, crashing to the floor.

Uncle Damien and Kurtis ran out of the front door in laughter. I was in tears. Aunt Stefani came over to aide me.

"Get away from me. You did it too, Stefani. I can't wait to tell Grandma what y'all did to me," I yelled.

"See, right there," she said. "This is what your little behind gets for always telling on us."

Kurtis and I fought like all brothers and sisters, but Kurtis took it a step further. I was nothing more than a little runt and he wanted me to be able to protect myself. I was so petite.

I wasn't taught how to fight like a girl would typically fight. No, I fought like boys would. This resulted in me being extremely tough as a girl. Anytime misunderstandings between friends and enemies arose, I had no fears. My sentiments during that time were: *No one was too big to be brought down to my size.*

"Just because you are small, Summer, doesn't mean you have to let anyone beat you," he scorned.

"I know," I told him. My head dropped as I looked down.

"Always keep your head up Summer. You hear me?" Kurtis would become angry with me if I didn't take him seriously.

"Yes," I said with tears filling my eyes.

Kurtis was my older brother. What was I going to say? In my eyes, he knew everything. Yeah, I followed his lead. So, like a fool I stood there fighting for dear life. Kurtis came at me with blow after blow … to my face, my head, and my body; I cried and fought my way out. Until one day; finally, I became tough enough where

I could back Kurtis into a corner—even if it was only for a hot, quick second!

Kurtis never knew it, but I always envied him, both he and my cousin Tina. They were both so limber and fast. I always watched them. I was too allergic to grass, allergic to food— allergic to everything! Most times, I could only just sit and watch them play and have fun.

I loved to run. I never could run for long however, due to my asthma. I wished I had speed as Kurtis had and I prayed that I could run and play as the other kids could. If having aliments weren't enough, I was just too darn prissy and much too small.

"Watch out Summer, you are going to get yourself hurt," everyone would say, as they shooed me away. I hated that. *Ugh.*

Kurtis was quick like a jack rabbit and his blows stung like a rattle snake. No way, was I messing around with him for too long before I bowed down. Kurtis was fast in everything he did. He was the best of the best; track, break dancing, skate boarding, and also as a quarterback in street football. Kurtis was my big bro!

Kurtis always won in the end. Of course, he was much stronger. He was also a savage when it came to handling karate nunchucks. No one could tell him that he wasn't Bruce Lee reincarnated.

My grandparents had their fair share of us during the summer months as well. Summers were always an adventure. One never knew what Grandma Maxine had in store. My mommy's mother and father were never married. Grandma Maxine did however, marry Grandpa Abe and my Granddaddy Charlie married Grandma Carolyn. They were all from the same small hometown.

Grandma Maxine was always doing things out of the norm. Although, she enjoyed many things just as her hometown friends and family did back home in Alabama, she also did a lot of out of the box thinking. She was interested in exposing us to museums, national parks and monuments, history, and opera. We had more books and pens and paper than one would find in a local book store.

If that weren't enough, oh how my grandparents loved to take road trips. Guess who their happy little passengers were? Yep, you guessed it, the two "partners in crime," Kurtis and Summer.

Car trunk loaded with a cooler full of fruit drinks, fresh fruit: peaches, plums, oranges, apples, and ham sandwiches, we were ready to roll. Grandpa Abe always had his front seat stash of snacks too, as backup. Lack of food definitely wasn't part of the road trip itinerary.

Summer trips were always fun—filled. Well, that was until our very first, grim encounter with racism. For the first time in our lives Kurtis and I were made to feel as though something was wrong with us simply because of our skin color.

On one particular day, Grandma Maxine took us downtown to shop. As we walked the sidewalks, we noticed white people began to cross over to the opposite side of the street almost as if their lives depended on it. You would have thought we had some type of contagious disease.

Hate was before our very eyes! The stares of hatred were uncomfortable and gave me chills. I grabbed onto grandma closely, seeking protection. I was so frightened. Welcome to grandma's good ole sweet, hometown in Alabama.

Grandma reassured me that all was going to be okay. "Summer, don't pay them any mind honey. That's just something you have to simply ignore sweetie," she told me.

A small town in Alabama that most people probably never even heard, of is where I, Summer found my family roots. Grandma showed me where our ancestors lived and how they once lived.

"An outhouse to use the restroom? What are you talking about grandma; they had to use the restroom outside?" I asked.

"You heard me Summer, they had to go outside."

My grandma pointed to the street sign above, "See, you see that sign Summer? That street is named after your great-grandfather."

I always thought granddaddy had a weird last name. Especially, being a black man. It all was beginning to make sense to me, finally. I remembered looking through a family photo album.

"Why is this white man's picture in our family album?" I asked.

My grandma replied, "Summer, that's your great-grandfather."

"But *he* is a white man grandma," I said.

"Yes Summer," my grandma replied. "Haven't you seen your granddaddy's sisters and brothers?" she asked.

"Yes," I replied. As I reflected, it dawned on me that that picture explained their hair texture and skin tone.

And that weird last name I had never heard of and could not recall another black person who had it.

"Who's last name is Oxford?" I questioned in a smart tone.

Eyebrows raised and shaking her head, Grandma Maxine just looked at me with a "Child please" expression on her face.

"Your granddaddy was a very fair skinned man before he came to work in Florida," she said. "Working in the sun all day made his skin turn four shades darker," she told me. On the other hand, Granddaddy Charlie's siblings resembled the famous singing family "*Debarge*." These gorgeous looking people, living in a small town like this—they appeared to be such misfits.

How many children have been blessed to meet and remember vividly their great-great- grandparents? Well, I did. After I met my Granddaddy Charlie's siblings, it was time to meet my Grandma Maxine's granddad.

It was time to switch gears and now meet my mommy's mother's side of the family. Grandma Maxine was anxious for us to meet her granddad. One would think this would be all so confusing for a young kid, but it wasn't. It had turned out to be the best trip in life ever! I had forgotten for a moment the racism that had taken place just hours earlier.

Once my eyes were on Grand Pop, I went into a state of awe. I was floored when our eyes met. There he sat, this American Indian man from the Cherokee tribe. He was no longer big in stature because he was old. Yet, the strength within him was still, very apparent.

"Red men" were what Indians were referred to and a red man with green eyes was what stared back at me. I could see my Great-Grandmother Willa in him. I instantly got chills just looking at Grand Pop. I knew at that moment that as long as the days are long, that image of him would live in my heart forever. As grandma drove up the long, red clay roads, my eyes graced the cotton fields. I was young at that time and did not realize the abuse, the agony, the struggle our ancestors faced when they were forced there. Many years later I came to the realization that some of my ancestors probably picked cotton from those same fields.

Sure, I was too young to completely comprehend what slavery meant. One thing for certain, there was this feeling of entrapment, a feeling of confinement; a feeling of unsettled spirits who remained, lurking in the thick country air.

Along the journey, we passed these big white houses with huge porches. The porches practically wrapped around the entire house. I knew my ancestors, even my grandmother worked in many of those homes raising the homeowners' kids. Cleaning and cooking for white families to receive their earnings was still, very common there in the state of Alabama for many African Americans.

We were not leaving Alabama until Grandma Maxine made it a point to show us Dr. Martin Luther King's house and church. She showed us the streets they marched on during the civil rights movement. Her eyes lit up with excitement as she explained her experiences with pride. She was proud to have been a part of change—a part of history; to have had a voice and stand for something. I could see how much it meant to her.

I remembered reading about Dr. King in school. To have been able to see the streets he walked, to visit the home in which he lived and the church in which he preached messages was empowering for me, even though I was a child. I couldn't wait to return home to share my pictures with my classmates for "show and tell" day.

Grandma Maxine planted some strong seeds in her grandkids that day and on that trip. How unlike the grandparents of today, who are trying to be as young as their grandchildren! I wonder what on earth they are enriching their lives with. What history are they imparting? What difference can they say they have made in the lives of their grandchildren, if any? What family roots and seeds are being planted? Seeds that many young kids are not privileged to experience in this day and age.

One of the largest cities in Alabama was a city that I admired. It made me want to succeed and attain wealth. We left the racism and separation of blacks in the small town to now seeing successful, prominent blacks in a large city. The blacks there owned the big white houses that other blacks worked in in the small town; this contrast of status fascinated me.

These city blacks had class. They were a class of people far different from what I had previously experienced. I am by no means saying that the "country folks" were any less, but the "city folks" had drive. They had dreams. Goals. You could see they had plans and strived to reach them. You saw results. For a young girl with dreams, that meant a lot.

My ancestors worked as maids and slaves in big homes just like these. But now, I walked over polished wood floors into large rooms, some rooms the sizes of entire homes. On top of that, these folks were relatives, they were my family.

"Wow," I said. My eyes were just amazed.

There was this one man who was drawn to me immediately. He was a sharp dresser. A good looking, distinguished gentleman. Bald headed, light complexioned man. He looked and smelled of money—a man of importance, a charmer, a fast talker.

Thinking back … I'm sure his roots were some place like Chicago or Detroit. He simply had that type of northern flavor and class.

"What is your name pretty young girl?" he asked.

"I'm Summer," I said, smiling from ear to ear.

"What a pretty name, Summer," he said.

"What's your name?" I asked.

"My name is Frank," he said.

Frank, I thought. *Frank*. The name rang through my head a few times. Mr. Frank reached out his hand to hand me something.

"This is a gift to you Summer that I want you to keep and remember me by." He reached out his hand to give me a silver dollar.

"Grandma, grandma hold on to this," I said. I ran as fast as I could over to her. "I don't ever want to lose this," I told her.

My cousins spoke proper English. Anyone could tell immediately that they were well educated men and women. I felt as though I had stepped into heaven, if only for a brief moment. I didn't want to leave. I remember looking out of the car window, tears in my eyes hoping one day to own a home like the ones I saw on that trip. Live in a big city like that. As grandma drove, I watched and watched until it all disappeared.

Even as a kid, a life of poverty wasn't something I wanted for myself. I wanted the best of the best in life.

As a kid, I traveled with grandma on a bus, on a train, on a plane, in a car. The only thing we missed was a boat. We missed travelling by boat. Given enough time, I'm sure grandma was going to arrange that one day also.

4

Daddy's Baby Girl

*I*n elementary school, I didn't feel pretty. I was as skinny as a toothpick. Aunt Stefani would say "You have beautiful eyes." But with the exact same breath, "I would hate to have your nose," she would say. At the time, I was too young to understand.

I thought, *Why would my aunt say something so mean to me?* She only had me by five years. I was her shadow. Everywhere she went I was there, sure to follow.

"Aunt Nat" short for Natalie, would say: *"Man you got some big ass lips!"* Now, she definitely was old enough to know better! Could it have been that she was somehow privy to the fact that, years later doctors would make millions enhancing womens' lips to emulate those same "big ass lips!"

I didn't cry. I sucked it up. Instead, I cried inside with confusion. I wasn't teased by my peers or classmates. No, I was being teased by my own family. I never questioned their genuine love for me. It was indeed, pure. Sure, they loved me to death, but their wicked sense of humor was totally unwelcomed. Maybe even a false sense of jealousy pierced the surface when my aunts' friends came around, especially their male friends.

My aunt's' friends always made a fuss about how pretty they thought I was. I was constantly mistaken for my Aunt Stefani's younger sister. I never saw what they saw in me. Neither did my aunts, or did they?

I recall my mommy once said, "Your Dad thought you should have been prettier as an infant." Being that my mommy had unique features; a long, thin nose similar to most white women, slanted eyes like that of an Asian persuasion and lips full like a Nubian Queen. She had the body like that of a swimsuit calendar model. Everywhere she went, the whispers followed as she walked by with grace.

I was a big baby, over eight pounds in weight. Hair covered my face. My complexion was red—as red as Georgia's red clay. The hair on my head when I was born was very fine and there was very little of it!

"Your Dad would get so upset when people would ask us if you were a boy," she told me.

Nonetheless, my daddy fell in love hard. I was his heart. He constantly reiterated to me how much love he had in his heart for me.

He would ask me over and over again, "Do you know that you are my heart sweetheart?" I would always gaze up in innocence and smile. Little did he know, we both had fallen deeply in love.

I was daddy's little princess. Everyone hated all of the attention he gave me. It wasn't my fault! Was that not how a Dad should feel towards his daughter? Shouldn't a Dad treat his daughter as though she was special?

As a daughter, should I not feel as though I could always rely on him as my blanket of security? My life was in his hands. He was my protector; to save me from the woes of the world I would soon face.

A daughter should already know what it is to experience love from a man. And that very first man should always be her Dad.

The Most Loved

A Faded Mirror

*D*addy's little girl was finally growing up. Looking in the mirror I could see my maturity beginning to take place. A little young lady had formed.

Sure, I could still see a strong resemblance of my daddy every single time I looked at myself. But, I could also see that I was no longer daddy's little sidekick; I stopped following him everywhere, I was ready to explore and get into my own trouble! It was time that I began to create my own stories.

Everyone in my family noticed that I was maturing physically. My boobs were the biggest thing on my small body frame. There was far too much breast for such a small young girl. *Lord, what am I going to do with all of this*? I often asked myself.

Yep, I had definitely entered into the mysterious "world of puberty." Boys had begun to pique my interest for sure. Not just any ole nappy headed boy was going to do … nope, my interest was strictly in smart, good looking and athletic boys.

Speaking of athletic, along came Richard who was my fantasy come true. Richard was from Mississippi; he was a good ole country boy, and he came from a very large family–twelve to be exact. A dozen different personalities and a dozen individual looks, but just enough resemblance to ensure they were indeed, siblings.

Richard was the baby of the family. Looking at him, he was far from country; he had the swagger of a traveled individual, ya know, as though he had been someplace in life other than the south.

Seeing Richard was like seeing my future; a future that I had once dreamed about somewhere during my long days and nights in "lala land." Once our eyes met, it was a wrap for the both of us. It was "love at first sight!"

Peeking through the curtains across the street, I glanced out of the window and I could see him standing there in the street. He was chattering with my cousins. He smiled as he looked up, only to see me looking at him through the window.

I could see Richard sizing up the fence. *Oh no, please don't.* I thought. He ran around in a circle and backed up as if he were a bull ready to strike and attack.

Next thing I knew, there Richard was racing towards the fence in an attempt to leap it.

"Please don't!" I yelled. I was indoors so there was no way he could hear me. I ran out of the house to see him lying on the ground. It was funny as hell, but I couldn't dare allow him to see me laugh.

"What on earth were you thinking trying to jump that fence man?" I asked.

"Well, I would have tried anything to get you to come out of that house and stop looking at me through the window," he said.

"Well, you didn't have to try to kill yourself to get my attention," I told him.

We both laughed. "Are you ok?" I asked. Richard just gazed up at me.

I stood there in admiration looking down at him. I had yet to see anyone like him before. In his facial appearance, he was every bit of a young man. But looking at his physique, he was all man. He was over six feet tall, and weighed heavy enough to run through the best athletes on a football field leaving them "dead on their behinds."

"You remind me of this woman on a poster I have up on the wall in my room," he said.

"Oh really?" I asked.

"Yeah, she looks like she's from the islands just like you do. She has your beautiful skin tone and pretty smile," he told me. I was there cheesing from ear to ear. His charm was definitely working.

Nervously, I stood there talking with him; but I knew that I was being watched. There was no way I should have been outside talking to any young boys. I was much too naïve. I had been much too sheltered to recognize any game that young boys played. Although, book smart … I wasn't one that would be called "street smart."

Lord, if word got back to Lex, my ass was grass for sure, I thought. Word definitely spread like a news alert on the ten o'clock news—before the sun could set and rise again. The news reporters, a.k.a. "my aunties," had a "news alert warning" addressed to Lex's ear.

It was on, the hunt to find Richard wouldn't come soon enough for Lex. He finally was right there, staring Richard face to face as he sized him up!

"Bang, bang … your black ass is dead! In my daughter's bed nigga, you won't be layin' your damn head! Negro stay away from my daughter! "You hear me?" he demanded of Richard. My daddy turned to face him. Only God knew what Lex Covington was contemplating inside of his head. May God help the person to whom his wrath was directed towards.

My daddy's eyes would change colors with his mood and anger was sure to ignite a change, almost instantly.

Good Lord, have mercy on us all. I thought. No one liked him when he became angry. For the record, that night, at that moment, Lex was fuming with anger.

"With all due respect sir, I won't be able to do that," Richard said boldly. No fear in his heart, Richard stood his ground.

"Boy, do you know how old Summer is?" my daddy asked.

"Yes, Summer is fifteen," he answered.

"It's 'Yes sir' to you Negro," my daddy snapped. "I don't know what you call yourself doing with my daughter, but it stops here tonight! Summer's mom and I are divorced now. But dammit boy, that doesn't mean that I don't have a say in what happens in my baby's life. Do you understand?" he asked.

Richard just stared with a blank face. "Does Summer's mom know about this?" Lex asked.

"I don't think so," Richard replied.

"Hear me boy, and hear me well–stay the hell away from my Summer!" he said firmly.

It was a cramped space inside the porsche. My daddy reached inside his glove compartment. He sat his gun holster down between the two of them.

"I can't do that, I have come to you as a man," Richard said.

"Yeah, that's the problem ... you are almost a man. My Summer is still my baby. Do you know how much Summer means to me?" Lex asked. Richard did not even have time to respond.

"She is my world." Lex said.

The fact that I didn't live with Lex allowed me to continue to communicate with Richard. My mommy had her own ground rules that she stood firmly on, but she was a little more lenient and merciful when it came to the household dating rules.

"Summer, if you exercise maturity, show me that you can maintain your grades and show respect for yourself at sixteen, and I will allow you to begin dating, understood?" she asked.

"Yes, I understand," I replied. *Thank you Jesus.* I thought to myself.

I was far from happy with the news, but at the very least Richard and I could still communicate via telephone and mail. Unlike my daddy, who wanted me to wait until college to begin dating, my mommy on the other hand, allowed me to accept phone calls from my friends. As long as the phone calls came in before seven o'clock, it was all good.

Our long distance courtship became expensive. Richard had a part-time job back home in Mississippi so he initiated the majority of the phone calls. I did the majority of the letter writing.

The days, months, and years came and went. Richard had college scholarship offers from across the country; literally, offers from coast to coast. He was recognized throughout his state as one of the top athletes. The newspaper clippings, trophies, and video clips from television all solidified his future for football fame.

"Summer, I love you. I can't imagine going off to college and someone else marrying you later," he told me.

"Richard, you have opportunities others wish they had," I said.

"I don't care what you say Summer, I'm not losing you. I'm willing to give it all up for you," he told me.

We were so damn stupid, young, and the dumb. We thought we knew everything. In actuality, we knew nothing. I was to blame as much as Richard was. How could I have allowed him to throw his life away for me? How could I have allowed him to depart from his childhood dreams? Instead, I should have convinced him that we could have made it without his sacrifices.

We were both scared shitless. We had grown so attached to one another. Neither one of us could have imagined life without the other. I would have died for Richard. He was my world and I was his.

I was being selfish. Agreeing to this foolishness of him throwing away such opportunities was simply insane–opportunities which meant a better lifestyle for his family as well. Hell, Richard was good enough to make it to the NFL, any day! And we threw it all down the drain for love.

It was an acceptable tradition in the south to marry young and have a house full of kids. The "house full of kids" however was never in our planned future. Shoot, Richard had enough nieces and nephews that we could borrow any of them, any time of day or night if what we really wanted was to "play house."

Richard made the decision to leave Mississippi and move to Florida prior to my graduation from high school. It was shortly after I graduated, that I felt I was too grown to abide by my parent's household rules. My mommy and now, my stepdad Joe, tried everything in their power to convince me what a grave mistake I was making.

My stepdad Joe had laid it out to me straight when he talked to me about boys. Boys were something that my own daddy and mommy were too afraid of to have a real conversation with me about. My mommy always tiptoed around the discussion, and Lex on the other hand, thought he'd just simply scare the living daylights out of any boy who would dare approach me.

Joe entered our lives after my parents divorced. I was still in elementary school at that time. He was a great provider. He would spend time playing board games with Kurtis and me. He made certain that we were included in the vacations he and my mommy took. Our weekends were often spent in the arcades at the beach, and ice cream was sure to follow any trip near the beach!

If anyone was going to give it to me straight, it was Joe. I trusted Joe. He always had our best interest at heart.

"Now you listen Summer, I know your mom doesn't really know how to talk to you about how things coexist between boys and girls and men and women, but I'm here to lay it out to you straight. The minute you get your first taste of a boy, you are going to lose your mind," he said.

And losing my mind was in fact, what I had done and then some! I thought I was ready to move out and get a place with Richard, so moving out was exactly what I did.

Little did I know how hard it was going to be. I missed my family badly. Richard and I decided to move northwest to a neighboring city away from where I grew up. To me it seemed like clear across the country. The first month was torture. The tears would flow every single evening.

Richard and I were living quite well to be a young couple. We had a nice apartment in a quiet, well-maintained community with a pool. But none of that mattered because I was miserably missing my baby brother, Skeeter. My mommy and Joe had a son together. He was simply beautiful. He was born with green eyes. We swore they gave her the wrong baby at birth. He had absolutely no color. He looked white and his hair was straight and fine too.

Skeeter's real name was Stephen, but we nicknamed him Skeeter. Skeeter simply skipped generations. He had our great-grandpa's eyes–those of the "red man" whose eyes I had looked into many years earlier.

Skeeter and I were thirteen years apart, but we were inseparable. Kurtis had already left the house and naturally, Skeeter grew closer to me by the minute. Although, he got on my last nerve and constantly did things to get me into trouble, he was still, "my little stinker." I was missing him like crazy!

Richard's family didn't have much so to them we were definitely living the good life. His family's home back in Mississippi was a very modest home. It was a wood-framed house with a screened front porch that needed lots of work. Beautiful flowers wrapped the front of the house along with a wooden loveseat swing on the lawn.

The neighborhood itself was nice. There were newer, model homes across the street from Richard's parent's house. Seeing where Richard had come from helped me to understand why he was so determined to create a new family life with me at such a young age.

A family was exactly what we both had made, far too soon.

"Richard, my menstrual cycle is like clockwork. I can time it by the hour. I'm pregnant," I whispered.

"Well, you're the one who was greedy and couldn't get your fast behind up. Well, I guess we'll definitely be getting married now," Richard smirked.

"We don't have to get married just because I'm pregnant!" I snapped.

"Summer, I've been asking for your hand in marriage for the past two years now. It's always the same excuse, you're too young." He said.

"I don't know what the future holds Richard," I told him. Richard and I had been together for the past four years and we were inseparable and now living together. But, I was a spoiled brat and I wasn't so confident that

Richard could provide for me and my child with the same lifestyle I had growing up.

Anything less than what I was accustomed to was beneath me. It was totally unacceptable. How was I going to tell my parents that I was pregnant? I had already moved out of the house far sooner than any young woman should have.

6

My Joy

"Summer, what are you doing here?" Grandma Maxine asked.

"Oh, it's nothing; just getting a checkup," I told her.

"Uh hmm," she said with raised eyebrows. I quickly looked away to avoid eye contact with her.

"Summer," she said again.

"Yes grandma?" I asked. She just looked over at me with curiosity. She knew there was something more, but what could she say? Her maternal instinct knew better! Why would I be at a clinic miles from where I resided?

"Alright Summer, I'll see you later," grandma said.

"Miss, you can go into 'Room 2,'" the nurse said. My eyes followed Grandma Maxine until she walked through the exit doors. I then proceeded to the examination room.

There was no need to confirm. I knew the damage was already done. The seed was firmly planted and rooted by that time.

"What are you here for?" the nurse asked.

"A pregnancy test," I replied.

The months had gone by fast and my health was the best it had been in my entire life. The allergic reactions, the asthma, the shortness of breath, there was no sign anywhere that any of it ever existed. It remained that way throughout my entire pregnancy.

I knew the moment I discovered I was pregnant that it would be a boy. In fact, I was overjoyed that it was a boy and I knew I would want to name him "Jaden." Having a girl, another "Summer," would have required far too much patience that I certainly wasn't capable of exercising at nineteen years old. Jaden, although not planned, was certainly going to be a welcomed addition to our lives.

Richard's marriage proposals came time and time again–many proposals, all leading to refusals over and over. Richard had had enough.

"If you don't know after all of these years of courtship, living together and now you being pregnant whether you want to be my wife, then, I won't ask you again!" he said.

I gained weight rapidly throughout my pregnancy. The more weight gained; the more I realized the delivery date grew shorter, and that Jaden would soon arrive. Jaden's soon coming arrival began to place the status of my relationship with Richard at the forefront of my mind. I could not fathom the idea of my first born being born out of wedlock. Yes, Richard was good to me. He was a hard worker and a loving man. I knew he would be a great father and husband.

The idea of being a single parent frightened me far more than being married to Richard ever could. After careful thought, I knew what I needed to do. One evening, I lit candles and placed them throughout the entire apartment.

"We need to talk babe," I told him. "Richard, I know you love me and have loved me since we first met. I love you and I want us to be a family. Richard, will you marry me?" I asked.

"Girl, what took you so long? Yes baby, I will marry you!" he replied. He was so excited. He would finally have his wife and now, a son; a son that he had given up his football career dreams to have.

The fact that I would live outdoors if I could ... I wanted anything but the traditional church wedding. There was no doubt that an outdoor wedding was what we would have.

It was early spring when we exchanged our vows. It took place so close to the gulf that we witnessed the waves as they danced ashore.

Our wedding was simple, yet so beautiful. White wooden chairs were aligned across the manicured grass. The decorated arch awaited me as my daddy escorted me to Richard and Pastor Smith. Everyone gathered around as the birds sang their praise of approval in the background. Lex released my hand and placed it up to Richard's.

On that day, my daddy appeared very, very sad and distant. I wasn't quite sure what was wrong. Lex, appeared to be somewhere; some place, anywhere other than present at my wedding.

"This man won't always look as handsome as he is today. For better or for worse ...." Pastor Smith quoted.

"I do," we both said in agreement.

"If you can't kiss her, you can't take her home," Pastor Smith told Richard. Man, talk about taking not only my breath away with that kiss–Richard was trying to make baby number two in the very presence of our witnesses as he saluted me!

After the birth of Jaden, Richard was the happiest man alive. To witness the birth of his first child and for him to be a boy was beyond words for him. Anytime he looked at Jaden he would get emotional and his eyes would fill with tears.

Little Jaden resembled both of us. You could definitely see each of us in him. As he aged, my features appeared more vividly in our son. My genes were much stronger than Richard's!

Richard vowed that he would work two full-time jobs if necessary to ensure I was able to stay home with Jaden until I felt comfortable leaving him with relatives and later, taking him to daycare. The years vanished before my eyes after the birth of Jaden until he reached toddler age. After that, the years flew by faster than the speed of light. Year after year, I witnessed Jaden being a happy, fun and loving kid. He didn't have a care in the world.

He had parents who adored him. That child didn't want for a thing. I recall Jaden's elementary school teacher saying, *"I've never seen a more polished child from head to toe in all my years."*

Family vacations, cookouts, you name it and Jaden was included. There wasn't much we did without our little man. He was our heart and soul. He made our family complete. There was nothing in the world we would not do for that little boy. Jaden was our pride and he was certainly the joy in our lives.

Our son was an entertaining kid. At our family gatherings he was the featured entertainment for visitors who would stop by quite frequently. If it weren't his dance moves, it was his laughter which was entertaining.

As Jaden grew, he played every sport. There was football, baseball and Jaden loved basketball. Richard never wanted Jaden to play basketball because he wanted him to perfect the sport of football. Anyone could clearly see Richard was trying to impose his failed dream of playing in the NFL into Jaden's future. He was intentionally prepping him; Richard was preparing Jaden to excel at being an exceptional quarterback.

7

A Time to Forgive

he work day had come to an end and it was
time to head home. I pulled my brand new
black SUV into the circular driveway of our home. I let
out a huge sigh. I took a moment to gather my thoughts;
I just sat there letting the cool air from the air conditioner
blow across my face.

*Forgiveness had become easy for me just as the
continual sins against me,* I thought. I sat there realizing
that I was indeed, a changed woman. I'd now become
blessed with what I had prayed for; agape love, God's
unconditional love. I then knew the saying was true: *"Be
careful what you ask for, you just may get it!"*

I fought back tears as I sat in the truck, thinking to
myself, *I don't want to go inside! What happened to that
smile that I had over eight hours ago? Where did it go?
Why did that smile leave once I arrived home?* I thought
about my son and I dried my eyes. I opened the truck
door and proceeded to the front door of our house.

Wow, those days of soul food aromas greeting me at the front door seemed so very long ago now. I literally shook my head hoping that those memories would disappear from my mind; they were too painful to remember. Holding on to the good times just wasn't enough anymore.

It's just not enough! I repeated to myself.

As disappointment and resentment built up inside me, somehow I managed to make a smile appear on my face to greet my family as I walked inside.

Richard mustered up a weak, "Hello...how are you?" in response to my smile.

"Hey pumpkin, how are you?" I asked Jaden.

I saw his head appear from around his bedroom door.

"Hi mom," said Jaden. He ran to give me a big hug as he jumped up into my arms.

"How was your day?" I asked Jaden.

"It was good Mom and how was your day?" he replied.

"It was fine son, just fine," I said.

"Love you Mom," Jaden yelled as he closed the front door heading outside to play.

I walked down a step into our sunken den and looked over at my CD rack full of gospel cds. There was nothing like praise music.

Hmmm ... *What shall I listen to this evening?* I thought. The music I selected blared inside the den, almost shaking the walls. I sunk into the plush, oversized leather couch and slid off my heels.

It was a must to change into something more comfortable in order to ensure a relaxing evening at home. The cold tile felt so good against the soles of my feet as I walked towards the master bedroom to remove my work clothes. As I walked into our bedroom, there lied Richard sprawled across the bed asleep, and as I suspected he had been home for hours.

"Isn't this something! I wish I could come home and just lay in the bed too," I said aloud hoping that he would hear me.

I made my way to the kitchen to prepare dinner. As I removed the dishes from the cabinets running the dishwater to rinse them, my body froze in time for a moment.

How did Richard and I get to this point in our marriage? Stevie told me we were heading here if things didn't change soon! I thought.

Stevie had already been through a divorce at a young age and he recognized all of the signs of divorce between Richard and me.

"Auntie, I love you and Unc," Stevie once told me. "I love you just as much as I love him. I don't want to see either of you hurt like this. Fix this," he urged.

In the same exact frozen daze, standing in the kitchen, my hands fell into the dishwater. I began to reminisce about all of the memories leading up to Stevie's death … Stevie and I could always talk about anything. I loved Richard's nephews (Stevie and Michael) as though they were my very own sons.

Stevie had been honorably discharged from the military. He asked to come live with Richard and me in order to gain a fresh start. Mississippi had no future for him so he knew he did not want to return home.

Stevie wanted a new beginning in order to provide a better life for his young daughters. Richard and I agreed to give Stevie this opportunity. We all agreed that Stevie wouldn't have to pay us any rent. Instead, we asked that he use his earnings to purchase a reliable vehicle and in time, prepare to get his own roof over his head.

God worked everything out in Stevie's favor as Richard was able to get him a job working at the medical equipment manufacturing and sales company he worked for. It was a Christian-based company with great pay and unbelievable benefits.

Richard and I were able to live extremely well by him working for such a great company. I also had great benefits and was receiving a good wage as well. Money was the least of our worries. It afforded us both an opportunity to help family members and friends who were in distressful situations; helping others was always in our nature.

In order for Stevie to finalize obtaining benefits from his new employer, it required him to return home to Mississippi and obtain his military discharge paperwork. Earlier, in the same week Stevie would have to return home to Mississippi, Richard and I went scouting for cars for Stevie. He was in dire need of transportation. We finally found a dealership, about an hour from our home that was willing to finance a vehicle for Stevie without requiring a co-signer.

At that time, Richard and I were home owners, we financed vehicles, had money saved, and we had credit cards and could thus, get anything we wanted with just our signature alone. We weren't willing however, to co-sign another vehicle and risk our credit worthiness.

We alerted Stevie of the dealership we found and arranged to take him there to look at their inventory. Immediately, there was one particular vehicle that caught his eye. It was all red, had low profile tires and had the engine of a powerful mustang in it; powerful and attention grabbing that car was.

Stevie was anxious to sign his life away on the dotted line. He deserved it. The vehicle fit him well. It was one sharp looking car. It fit his personality to the "T". Stevie himself was an extremely handsome young man. And I do mean extremely. He was a head turner.

But, what was most appealing was Stevie's gentle soul. A loving and kind young man; his weakness however, was women—like most men. But, that never stopped him from preferring a relationship over the single life; he was a responsible man.

My cousin Kim's son, Aaron, lived in Mississippi also and had come to visit with Jaden for the summer (Aaron and Jaden were the same age). Stevie, being the kind-hearted and thoughtful man that he was, volunteered to take Aaron back home with him when he went to get his discharge papers.

We pitched the idea to Kim and she also felt Stevie was responsible enough to entrust him with Aaron.

"I want to go. Can I please go?" yelled Jaden.

I brushed off the thought of Jaden leaving me to go out of the state. I was not comfortable with Jaden staying at a friend's house or even a relative's house in town … yet alone going away on a trip without me in the car, no way!

"No way, Jaden!" I told him.

Immediately, I heard God's voice whispering in my ear … *"He's my child, when are you going to trust me with him?"* I disregarded His voice. While riding back from finalizing all of the paperwork for the vehicle with Stevie, Richard began to talk with me about Jaden wanting to take the trip with Stevie.

"Richard, Jaden is just too young," I told him.

"Summer, we have to let go at some point," Richard said.

"It's too soon," I said. Fear, anger and frustration filled me quickly.

God's voice again, *"You trust me with everything except Jaden, aren't you the one who gave Jaden back to me? It's time you trust me with Jaden, this is your test! How much do you trust me? This is your test of faith!"* I could repeatedly hear God speaking to me softly.

Not Jaden, I thought. Tears filled my eyes.

"Yes Jaden!" God's voice said to me again. My heart filled so heavily with fear at that moment. I rode in the truck in complete silence the rest of the way home from the dealership. There may have been silence in the

truck, but there was a full blown conversation going on between the Lord and me in my head.

"Do you know how you feel for Jaden, Summer?" God asked. *"I feel stronger than you feel. God spoke to me. I died for you and Jaden. It's time you trust me with Jaden, I am a jealous God,"* He said. Very few words escaped from me for the rest of the evening. I isolated myself from everyone that entire night.

Looking at Jaden, that child was my pride and joy … I couldn't imagine life without him in it. *It's not that I don't trust you Lord, I don't trust people and circumstances!* I said to myself.

"I am that I am," said God.

Enough said, I thought.

Didn't I realize that God controls everything? He could have struck Jaden dead at six years old at that very moment … right before my very eyes because he is GOD! Jaden walked into the room and snuggled up underneath me.

He hugged me and kissed me lovingly, "Mom, I really want to go," he said.

I looked down into Jaden's big, dark eyes, "What a beautiful child God has blessed us with," I said aloud.

"Jaden, you can go to Mississippi," I said. He jumped up and down dancing across the ceramic tile floors. Jaden became ecstatic prompted by me finally agreeing that he could go on the trip. No, it hadn't been Richard's decision everyone was awaiting, but solely mine and mine alone. I was the one who gave birth to that child. It was my decision.

The car loaded and ready to go, I waved goodbye to Jaden as I watched the car travel down the road until I could no longer see them anymore.

Richard comforted me, "It's going to be okay Summer."

"I know, I must trust God," I replied.

In a deep sleep, the phone rang and woke up Richard. "What?" yelled Richard. "Dead?" he exclaimed. "Stevie is dead??"

I leapt out of my sleep and landed across the room alongside Richard's side of the bed. I held onto every word that proceeded from Richard's mouth from that moment on....

"Where is Jaden?" I frantically asked Richard. Pacing, I began to cry and scream. "Where is my child? Richard, where is my child?" I cried. Searching clothing, I grabbed anything to throw on to try to dress myself. I looked around the bedroom for either of our car keys.

I spotted a set of keys on the dresser. Richard's eyes met mine.

"He's okay Summer. Jaden, is fine," he said.

"I don't believe you!" I cried.

"Jaden is with your cousin Kim," Richard assured me.

My hand and fingers were shaking nervously as I dialed Kim's number. "Where are Jaden and Aaron, Kim?" I asked.

"They are both here with me asleep Summer," she said. "What's wrong with you girl?"

"I don't know what is wrong—all I know is that we received a call saying that Stevie is dead and we are on our way to Mississippi," I told her.

"What? Alright, well I have Jaden here with me and I'll see you when you arrive," Kim said.

"Please have Jaden call me the minute he gets up," I told her.

"Ok bye Summer," Kim said. Stevie was Richard's sister's first born. I can't imagine what she must be going through right now. Hell, Stevie was like a son to us both!

It hit me. *Stevie is dead!* I ran out of the side door into our backyard and let my sorrow be released into the air. I needed air to help me breathe. It hurt so deeply. My knees fell to the ground onto the slab of concrete where our tool shed was located. I cried and cried and cried until there were no more tears left.

Returning inside, I didn't see Richard anywhere. Yet, I heard his sobs. Richard was solid and a strong man in stature, but at that very moment, he was more like a helpless infant. He didn't care if I saw him in his weakness. He laid his head into my lap and wept like a little child who had lost his way home.

My Lord, where is Michael? was my next thought. Michael was Stevie's younger brother. They were inseparable. Michael had also come to live with us for a brief spell, but his experience was unlike Stevie's. He was very irresponsible and was more of a burden. His stay was short lived because the more we tried to help him, the more lost he became.

I knew better than to ask Richard if Michael also was in the vehicle. Those two were inseparable. I couldn't imagine Michael not being in the car too.

Lord, please spare us Michael. Please don't let Michael have been in the vehicle too. I prayed. For the moment, I said nothing concerning Michael.

I knew Richard had very few details at the time. Much was due to the fact that they knew we would be on the road highly emotional while driving to get there. All Richard had been told was that Stevie had lost control of his vehicle, killing himself, and two others. We received phone call after phone call from Florida and Mississippi— all relatives calling us in disbelief!

We were on the cell phone almost our entire drive. Finally, we simply silenced the ringer; we had no more answers to all of the questions we were being asked. We no longer had any comfort to offer other grieving family members. There we were together, but feeling so helplessly alone.

Nothing or no one could have prepared us for what we were about to face. We never imagined Stevie's death, let alone such a tragic one. Before we arrived at the scene of the accident, we previously contacted the local sheriff's deputy who was conducting the investigation and we requested that he meet us there.

The deputy greeted us with sympathy in his eyes.

"Ma'am, sir," he said.

"Thank you officer for coming," Richard said.

"I must warn you both, there is still evidence here at the scene," he said. We walked around the small tree where Stevie's vehicle had wrapped itself around. There was body tissue and blood surrounding the tree. I ran away with my face covered in tears. I couldn't bear the thought of Stevie's last moments.

"I would like to see the vehicle please," Richard said. The vehicle wasn't far away from the scene of the accident. "Can you please explain what on earth happened here?" he asked.

"Apparently, the driver was driving home from the club in the early hours of the morning. At some point, he lost control and ran off of the road hitting the tree," he said.

"It has been confirmed that in addition to Stevie being dead, his best friend Keith and his cousin Nick are also deceased," said the deputy.

"This is too much! Where was Michael?" I cried.

"Michael is the deceased's younger brother?" the deputy asked.

"Yes sir, it is my understanding that there were four people in the vehicle," I told him.

"This is true, however the other person wasn't identified as Michael," he said.

"Then, who?" asked Richard.

"It was a friend who is currently in the hospital in critical condition. Witnesses said they saw them all before they departed the club's parking lot. They stated that Michael had opened the car door to get in when someone called him to get into another car instead.

Again, my condolences to your family. I'm very sorry," said the officer.

Richard's sister Linda (Stevie's mother), had already given permission for us to handle everything; the accident, the funeral arrangements, everything. Richard, Linda, along with Stevie's ex-wife, (the mother of his beautiful daughters), and I all gathered at the funeral home to take care of the arrangements. Both families decided to have the two cousins' funerals together at the local school's auditorium. The best friend's funeral however, was held in his hometown a few towns over.

The entire community was humbled by the tragic accident. Everyone gave such overwhelming support to both families. The going home services were beautiful. That day was a day of celebration—something so tragic actually saved souls.

There were young men, old men, young women, boys and girls on that day that made a conscious decision to dedicate their lives to Christ. None of the lives lost were lost in vain. There was a purpose. A life for a life; another life for two more lives, and a final life in order for more lives to be saved. No, God indeed, had a masterful plan. On that day, it was time to forgive.

8

A Different Me

Returning home, we both dreaded opening up Stevie's room door and sorting through his belongings. His smell, along with the idea that we would no longer witness that beautiful, big smile, changed the atmosphere in our home. It was dark. It was cold. It was hollow within the walls of our home.

Jaden was sad. He didn't quite understand it all. We tried our best to explain.

"God loved Stevie best son. He was ready for him to come home. He only allowed him

to visit with us for a brief time," I whispered.

"But, I will miss him," Jaden said.

"We all will," I replied. I smiled at Jaden.

I held him tight until he said, "Mommy, I can't breathe." I didn't want to let him go.

Richard isolated himself from us. He was filled with anger. He was bitter. He was resentful. He had become instantly depressed upon our return home. He was absent; both mentally and physically from us. Nothing seemed to matter anymore. Not me. Not Jaden. Not our home. Our family became separated. When Stevie died, it was as if Richard died right along with him.

"Richard, I am hurting too! Driving home yesterday from work, my mind went into a trance. I no longer saw the cars. I heard the devil whispering in my ear … *'Drive your truck off of the bridge. You are losing your mind, life isn't worth it.'* All of those thoughts the devil tried to put in my head Richard! But then, God spoke to me and said *'you have life'* Summer, and Jaden needs you. Your family needs you too!" I demanded.

Richard simply looked at me with a blank stare. He was oblivious. He became disengaged from our finances. It no longer mattered if our home had the most manicured lawn on our block. He was simply existing.

He was no longer living life as he once did so freely, so effortlessly. His attire was unimportant. He no longer coordinated his wardrobe. He embarrassed Jaden and me constantly when he escorted us to the malls.

I contacted Richard's older brother to seek out some support for Jaden and me. "Barry, I really need someone to help me with Richard," I said.

"What's going on, Summer?" he asked.

"Since Stevie's death, I don't know who my husband is anymore," I told him.

"What is he doing?" Barry asked.

"Nothing Barry, Richard does absolutely nothing and I mean nothing! He walks around sad and angry all of the time. He's no longer a husband to me neither is he a dad to Jaden. We are losing him fast," I cried.

Night after night I cried out to the Lord. Richard no longer anointed Jaden's head nor my head as he had done every morning before leaving the house. He no longer prayed over our home. Spirit after spirit entered our home week after week and he no longer cast them out. Instead, it was as though I was fighting Richard's depressed and lustful spirits alone.

After time, I could no longer sleep in the same bed with Richard. I felt violated. He no longer caressed my body as a loving husband should. The prepared, warm baths and full body massages became rough aggressive sex instead. *Why had my nights become so restless?* I wondered.

His words became much harsher—they pierced my body like a sharp sword entering an already sore wound. It was as if he now took pleasure in seeing me in pain. He delighted in my suffering, but why? What had I done that was so wrong that my husband had become so disgusted with me as his wife?

I did all of the things that a loving wife should. I adored his family and friends; even though several of his sisters hated my guts, why? Because I was pretty, slim and smart!

It was as though I was "sleeping with the enemy" in the dark, wandering the wilderness, or forest in fear of the next strike. I slept with one eye opened. Often, after finally dozing off, I would awaken to find Richard staring down at me.

Unbeknownst to me, I had begun talking in my sleep. Richard had become the court reporter. He transcribed every word "which proceeded out of my mouth." It was those lustful spirits that were somehow allowed into our bedroom. *Was that the demise of our marriage? Was it Stevie's death?* I kept going back from one explanation to the other … searching and searching for answers.

Perhaps, what I was experiencing was spiritual warfare, I told myself. I remembered the night I felt someone or something touching my skin, but there was no one in the room with me. It all came back to my remembrance … one night I felt the crawl of the sheets lifting slowly, proceeding from my legs up to my vagina. That spirit engaged my entire body. I was frozen, as if someone had both hands lifted above my head and my ankles tied.

I felt hot with an intense sensation. I awoke feeling violated by someone other than my husband. I recalled as a young child, overhearing my great-granny speaking to an adult about a similar violation, but I was too young to fully comprehend at that time.

Our bedroom had become a battlefield of lusts–those forbidden and those that were hidden. *Those spirits weren't yours Summer,* I convinced myself. They were unfamiliar spirits—I didn't recognize them.

I felt heavy breathing on my neck, heat around my face. My sexual behavior remained normal; consistent with what I had grown accustomed to. However, Richard's behavior became very controlling and downright nasty! Richard's requests for me to perform acts that I was neither willing to perform nor desired to perform was unsettling.

No! It was Richard. I was convinced. Richard was the one who began to touch me; in a way that a man would handle a woman that he didn't love, or care about. Instead, it had become rough and undesirable. He didn't seem to care, that left me crying afterwards.

What had happened to my beloved Richard? Who took away the man that would call in sick from work just to make love to me all day long? I wanted that man back! I hadn't signed up for this new man that had surfaced. I would have left his ass right then and there had I known this was what my married life would become. *Did I see this coming? Was this why I was so afraid to marry Richard initially?* I thought.

Give it time Summer, things will get better. I hoped. No, things didn't get better! Each day became progressively worse. Somewhere, somehow, he forgot his beautiful family—Jaden and me. We had become strangers living in his new world.

Whatever was going on in Richard's life, really didn't have anything to do with Jaden or me. I didn't quite understand it at the time. Truth be told, I didn't understand it at all. I was oblivious to what had happened to us and the reality of us "living the good life."

Whatever Richard had been going through had nothing to do with his family, but everything to do with his relationship with God. God had a bone to pick with Richard. I was certainly happy that I wasn't him. The sad reality of it all was that Jaden and I suffered most. I protected Jaden as much as I could from seeing the changes in his Dad, but I could only for so long.

Richard had done something very wrong in the sight of God and I felt it every single time he laid down beside me at night. It made my skin crawl in fear. Out of the day's twenty-four hours, I prayed every second, minute, and hour that I could in an attempt to regain my family.

Love making was out of the question. Instead, I felt like a street walker who had been released of her duties by her pimp.

"Richard you are hurting me, stop it!" I screamed. I cried as he stroked me long and hard. It was as if he wasn't even in the same room with me. I tried with every ounce of strength I had to push him off of my body, but there was no use. He was as heavy as a tree stump. I remember a night when his eyes were bloodshot as he looked down at me; a look of pure evil. He simply grunted and continued pleasing himself inside of me.

I had had enough. I removed my belongings from our master bedroom into our guest bedroom, the room where Stevie once slept. Fortunately for me, we had redecorated the entire bedroom with light colors to give the room an uplifting appeal. Still, I don't know how I even managed to get Richard to agree to paint that room .... I tiptoed in at night so Jaden wouldn't notice me leaving our bedroom to sleep in the guestroom. It had become my place of "sanity." It was the only place in the house where I could escape reality.

Jaden was growing up. He was no longer that toddler who kept us entertained with his humor. He was one sharp kid. He was quick on his toes and ready to come at you with something totally unexpected and at any given moment.

After Stevie died and before I moved in, we decided we would use that room primarily as a prayer room; our "prayer closet" if you will, for times when Richard or I wanted to spend time alone with God. Although, I was no longer sure what Richard's relationship was with God all the same, I continued to respect his time alone when he was in the room. However, anytime I chose to enter the room, there was absolutely no respect.

It was, *"I need to see you in the bedroom— when are you going to finish?"* He would ask. Or, *"Summer, get the telephone,"* He would say. I would become furious because I never disrespected his time alone with God. I always ensured that Jaden, the phone, visitors, me— absolutely no one, disturbed him during his time in the "prayer closet."

My marriage was becoming completely unglued, but somehow, through our bible studies, God was performing a magnificent work by using me to help counsel other married women.

"Richard, I don't know what God is doing through your wife, but, my wife isn't the same since she has been studying with your wife," Donnie said.

"God isn't using Summer to do anything," I heard Richard reply snappily. When I heard those words I was devastated.

Donnie was Richard's best friend. His wife Melanie had a reputation of being loose with men. Richard and everyone else were quite aware. Yet, everyone acknowledged and respected the fact that Donnie was committed and wanted his marriage to work.

Melanie, wanted change, she simply didn't know how to go about it. It was apparent she was dealing with strong holds that penetrated her deeply. Her change definitely wouldn't come over night. It was going to take fasting, praying and casting out spirits, but, we all were prepared to help Melanie through it.

Our bible study group was filled with mostly young couples. We were powerful in the word and our street evangelism ministry, which had a mission to help the homeless, was going strong. What we couldn't accomplish by the word alone, we would accomplish through our giving. Month after month, we gave many of our prized possessions to the homeless.

We would consistently take bags of clothing, bed comforters, pillows and sheets to them. We would even have cookouts in local parks to gather them around and then, minister the Word to them. Our mission was not to force the Word on them, but to show them God's love in us through our giving and support. We were there to listen and encourage them. We wanted to give them hope in knowing that there is someone above who is truly looking out for them.

Week after week, the ministry became my escape. The more people visible; the more people witnessed Richard's distaste for me when he was in my presence. I couldn't understand it. I was a hard-working and loving wife, a great mother, friendly to everyone, supportive; I loved and cared for my husband. *What was I doing wrong?* I wondered.

How could a man who once showered me with the world, who gave me a week's wardrobe every month, prepared candlelight dinners, took me away for weekend getaways, purchased anything I wanted for our home, raced home to prepare dinners for our family, kept the outside of our home immaculate, and who was extremely romantic, the best dad a mother could wish for, and who knew every touch to make me melt in bed–how could this same man become so cold-hearted, disrespectful, and obnoxious towards his wife?

What we once shared was a partnership; whatever Richard was willing to do for me, I was also willing do to for him and then some. It was always reciprocated.

"How could this become my life now, Lord? I've been so faithful Lord," I said. I saw my family being ripped apart piece by piece. The more I engulfed myself in God's word, the worse our marriage became.

Not many knew the state of my marriage therefore, sympathy and compassion was not something that was given liberally.

"Why am *I* here supporting my brother during his sermons and *you* aren't here with your husband Summer?" Vivian asked.

Not that I owed Vivian's bipolar ass any explanation, I replied, "When my husband can live at home, the life that he is preaching to others, then, and only then, will I be there. I'm not going to be a hypocrite!" I snapped.

I was mistaken to think that Vivian and I had actually formed a close relationship. It had become very apparent that when it came to her baby brother, right or wrong, her support was solely for him.

"I refuse, and hear me clearly, I refuse to mislead anyone's congregation into thinking my marriage is solid." I told her.

"Well now …." Vivian said.

"Well," I interrupted I must go now. Enjoy the sermon now, goodbye Vivian," I told her.

After all of the reflections (Stevie's death, my marriage, the ministry) I had in the kitchen … the next day, I found myself in the corner of the break room at work, whispering, so no one could hear me—my voice trembled.

"Yes, I am having a very hard time coping with my life right now. I really need to speak with someone. I understand this service is to help employees find doctors in their area?" I asked.

"Yes ma'am, everything is strictly confidential, this service is provided through your employer. We will find you the help you need," said the concerned young man on the other end of the phone.

Talking to Debra was like having a conversation with one of my girlfriends. I selected Debra from the list of available counselors. Yeah, I did right choosing a female counselor. I doubt a male would be very sympathetic to the idea of me leaving my husband!

I was told I was eligible to receive five free visits and if additional visits were deemed necessary, my health insurance would cover those expenses.

A shrink? Wow, has it really gotten to this extent? I thought. I never thought in a million years, that I, Summer, would be on a couch telling a perfect stranger about things I previously only trusted to share with God. Debra was different though.

Debra and I shared the same beliefs … she was also a Christian, a mother, a friend, a strong African American woman like myself. I felt very comfortable telling Debra all of my fears, hopes, and about my existence, now a complete "disaster zone."

"You're not doing anyone any favors by holding everything in, Summer," Debra said.

She can't tell anyone else my personal affairs unless I was at risk of harming myself or others, so why not release this heavy burden? I asked myself.

"Summer, you really need to stop holding everything inside of you and then, exploding like a bomb later," She told me.

Little did Debra know … in my younger days, I was "Lex, Jr." My temper was uncontrollable! The current state I was in was actually a much more controlled place of peace and calm. No one could get hurt physically or emotionally if I remained reserved and calm, so I thought.

"You enjoy writing?" Debra asked.

"Yes, I enjoy it immensely," I said.

"Well, why don't you try journaling," she suggested.

Paper and pen in hand, I began to write ... *'If he says he loves the way I am ....'* Wow! There really is something to this writing! *Man, I haven't done this in years.* I thought. It felt really good to just write how I was feeling. I felt so light, so free ... I feel like a little girl again, racing around the driveway on my "green machine" *zoom, zoom, zoom* ....

A heavy burden had been lifted indeed. *Why, didn't I think of this myself?* I thought. I looked up at Debra confused. A look similar to one an innocent daughter would give her mother when she hears *"No! You can't wear your favorite spring dress outside because it's winter!"* I mean yes, I did get what my counselor was saying, but I would need far more than just this journaling to get me through my life right now. I needed direction and I needed answers.

I had lost my identity somewhere. I didn't know where to turn to find it. How would I pick it back up once I found it? I had done everything "The Good Book" said I should do. I no longer cursed, I hadn't listened to rhythm and blues in seven years, I didn't go to clubs, I didn't watch "R" rated movies, I was exercising the most holy life possible. *Why had I become so unhappy?*

Growing up, I had always heard: *"One can become so heavenly minded that they are no earthly good."* I never quite understood what that truly meant until I arrived there myself. "No earthly good" is exactly where I was, no good to anyone anymore; not myself, especially. I had lost my true identity through being the minister's wife, being Jaden's mother, the sister-in-law, the big sister, the daughter, the friend, the co-worker.... Where was Summer? What did Summer want for Summer?

I repeatedly begged and pleaded with Richard to seek help; for us both to go to counseling. Oh, we finally went to counseling alright as a couple, but it was far too late!

"Unfortunately, you are both too far gone in your marriage to restore it," the counselor said bluntly.

Richard was the one who had chosen this particular counselor and yet, the counselor had not agreed with him that there was actually any hope for our marriage. Although, Richard was making all of the mistakes, he surprisingly wanted our marriage. We both exited the doors with stone faces. There was no emotion from either of us. There was absolutely nothing else positive that could have been etched into our future upon our departure from the counselor's office that day.

Richard's vicious cycle continued to play out week after week in our home. Richard would do well for a week or two and then, it was back to encountering his mean and evil spirits. He no longer greeted me with any acts of kindness. His words were no longer soft spoken and gentle. Instead, they were abrasive and they were slicing across my heart daily.

How could a man who once knew how to love me "as Christ loves the church" torment me in such a manner? If you're sick, you go to the doctor and seek help. If you're hurting, again, you seek help. Richard had always, always, leaned and depended on me for support.... Why did he now refuse to talk to me? There was no longer any communication between us. I no longer trusted him. I didn't recognize him as my husband any longer; as the father of my son, as my soul mate. He had become a total stranger.

Jaden didn't witness the arguments between Richard and me as he got older. I was very careful to keep him away from us anytime we argued. He was still the happy go lucky kid he had always been. He never wanted for anything and would go about his every day routine without a care in the world. Why should he have had a care at his age? He needed to enjoy his childhood and be allowed to do what children do … just live life and be free!

Every night I cried myself to sleep. I was so unhappy. All the years Richard and I were together, I never gave any notice to another man longer than a split second. There was never a second glance. I always kept myself sexy and well-kept for Richard. My feelings were changing day by day. I no longer rushed home from work. Instead, I buried myself in work, finding reasons to work overtime so that I didn't have to come home to face Richard.

Any time Richard would be late coming home, there was such a warm and peaceful atmosphere within the house. The minute he returned however, it seemed to become artic cold. Below freezing temperatures seemed to follow him through the doors. I really don't know what happened to Richard. I don't know if it was Stevie's death that uprooted something already hidden deep within him. Either way, I knew I would lose my complete mind if I continued to stay in the same house with him.

"Richard, we need to talk very soon," I said. I called him on my lunch break to advise him that I would be home on time that evening. "It is imperative that we carve some time out soon to sit down without Jaden and have a conversation," I told him.

"Okay Summer," He said. In his heart, he had to have known what I was preparing myself to tell him. That entire week, the week prior to that conversation, I isolated myself from the family and stayed in my prayer closet.

"I need permission Lord! I can't defy your word and leave my husband without your consent," I prayed.

I cried. I prayed. I cried more tears and I prayed even more. I also reached out to my prayer warrior who was one of Richard's other sisters. Vicky helped pray for my strength to endure and for guidance and direction for her brother to find his way and salvage what was left of his family. She cried with me. The Lord knew, Vicky loved us all and it hurt her just as much to see our family in such ruins. Word eventually spread throughout Richard's family about our issues.

I knew Richard's older brother, Jesse long before I ever laid eyes on Richard. Jesse was crazy about some "Summer." He adored me. He couldn't stand by and watch our marriage be destroyed without doing his job as an older brother, yet alone as an elder of a holiness church. Once news of our failing marriage reached Jesse, he and his wife, Pat, drove down to Florida to stay with us for an extended trip. Their intent was to minister and counsel us without Richard finding out their true intentions.

Well, Jesse and Pat's arrival was at the most inopportune time in Richard's eyes. Normally, Richard would simply be elated to see his brother Jesse and his sister-in-law. Yet, this time, there was no love when they arrived that day. Richard barely greeted them. Instead, he was busy chewing my behind! And for what?

I can't even recall what set him off that day. Whatever it was, there was no cause for him to speak to me in that manner. To add insult to injury, it happened in front of family. That was embarrassing to say the least.

"Man, have you lost your mind Richard? Come here man!" Jesse told him. Jesse pulled Richard aside and spoke to him in another room.

Jesse eventually stormed out of the room. He immediately pulled me aside and said to me in front of his wife Pat, "I am a man of God and I don't believe in divorce. But, I do know what I have witnessed is not of God. I would be less of a man to advise you to stay with my brother under these conditions. Summer, you don't deserve this and my heart goes out to you. I can't advise you what to do. Just know that you don't have to stay here!"

"I'm sorry Summer, but we won't be staying here this trip with the two of you," Jesse said. I walked them both to their car.

"I'm very sorry Jesse and Pat," I said.

"Not as sorry as we are for you Summer," Pat said.

"We will be praying for you Summer," Jesse said.

"Thank you," I said. I felt a warm, single tear drop on my face.

I hated the thought of what awaited me indoors. All I knew was that I had to face it head on!

"Lord, either I am going to be in a mental institution or one of us will end up dead!" I said. *One of us may snap!* I thought to myself.

It was apparent, in some form or fashion, that Richard had violated the vows of our marriage sexually. Or, that God had to deal with him by removing me out of his life. Either way, what we were going through had nothing to do with me, but everything to do with Richard. I didn't have a clue why, when, or how, but I knew it wasn't about me.

"Richard, I don't have to tell you ... you already know what I'm getting ready to say. I'm leaving you Richard. I'm not saying I want a divorce but, I want you to get help and find the man I once knew," I said.

He sat there with little emotion. "You take my son and I will kill you!" he said, looking me dead in my eyes.

At that very instant, my mind immediately went back to the moment when Prophetess Williams spoke prophecies over my life. Our lives had never crossed paths before yet the week prior to us meeting, I remembered feeling a sense of urgency that individuals were wishing harm to come into my life.

Prophetess Williams "didn't know me from Eve"— she didn't know anything about me nor anything about what I was going through with Richard. She knew nothing! Oddly enough, when I was in the prophetess' presence, she was extremely distant with me. She was kind, polite and cheerful with everyone else in the room, except for me.

My personality type was cheerful, like a butterfly. I found it quite odd that she would treat me that way. After all, we didn't know one another. I proceeded to get up in an attempt to leave the room when she arose and prophesied.

"I see a coffin and blackness all around you!" She said. I stopped immediately in my tracks and stared at her. I hadn't told anyone what I had been feeling in my spirit the week before.

"There are four women who wish you death!" She described every single one of the women to me. Ironically, I was able to identify each of them. In my heart, I already had an idea who these women were before she spoke this prophecy over me.

"Have no fear. I don't know why I keep seeing Psalm 23, but you know why," she told me.

Yes, I knew exactly why. I had been reciting the Psalm day in and day out for the past week.

"No harm shall come upon you! Although I see coffins ... I also see angels surrounding you. Precious, there are so many angels surrounding you ... your enemies can't get near you! Remember, God has His watch over you ... you are protected," she assured me.

I knew God had me covered. It was the confirmation that I needed to move forward and moving forward was exactly what I intended to do. I was leaving Richard, threats and all. God had my life in His hands.

Yes, it was a "different me!" Never would I, Summer, have had the courage to leave the only man who meant the world to me. I owed it to myself to find out who Summer really was because I could no longer depend on Richard's love.

It was time I discovered the true meaning of self-love, without my family's involvement, without Richard's family, without friends. I needed to know the real Summer! *Who is she? Who was Summer Covington?* I had to find her ....

9

Forsake Thee Not

usic filled the room as I ran a warm, bubble bath. *Ahhh, this water is just what I needed today.* I thought as I slumped further down into the bathtub. My mind unscrambled the earlier work day as the music I put on began its wonderful works of massaging the stress away. I was mentally drained. Peace, finally!

I played with the soap suds on my now thin legs. *Wow, I can't believe this.* I thought to myself. I wanted to lose some weight … maybe about fifteen pounds, but somehow, I've managed to lose about thirty pounds instead. *How did that happen?*

All of the stress. If the wind blew too hard, I surely would have been tossed away. My wardrobe of designer business suits all swallowed me up now; I went from a solid size twelve to a size four in just a matter of a few months. *How was that possible?*

If another person asks me if I'm sick I am going to scream! I thought. *Yes, I'm sick alright ... I'm sick of y'all heifers asking me the same stupid question over and over again! Relax Summer... relax!* I told myself. I finally began to relax and meditate a little. It was exactly what my mind, body and soul had been craving the entire day ... peacefulness.

And then, the phone rang ... and it rang again, and again.

"Ugh," I said. I grabbed a towel and ran into the kitchen to answer the phone on the wall. "Hello," I said.

"Hello, how are you doing today?" Richard asked.

"I'm fine Richard," I answered feeling irritated.

"Is everything ok with Jaden?" I asked.

"Yes, Jaden is fine Summer. When are you coming to pick him up?" He asked.

"On the day we agreed!" I snapped. "Listen, I really need to go Richard!" I told him while at the same time hanging up the phone. My entire demeanor had completely changed from that of tranquility to depression–I suddenly felt deeply depressed.

Richard could take me to my boiling point; in a matter of seconds. He knew exactly the right buttons to push, the right words to say. He knew which elements to use in order to ignite the chemistry within my body to create a mad frenzy.

Yes, it only took a matter of seconds! Although physically apart, mentally, Richard was very capable of toying with me; he had me as if I were a puppet on a string. He could toy with my brain at any given moment. My emotions were like soft clay in his hands; used to create something and then, destroy it. The minute I deciphered his voice, the puppet show would immediately begin for him. He enjoyed every minute of it. I could tell because I knew him so well.

I was confused as to why God would allow me to continue to go through such painful emotions with that man, such profound agony. It didn't take long later that night before my anger grew stronger. Resentment and distrust developed. I became angry at God.

"How could you God? I adored you, I worshipped you! I ate, breathed, and slept you. I was in your presence morning, noon, and night. I gave you my everything! Remember me, Summer? Your faithful servant, remember me? Do you?" I asked.

I tried to make sense of all that was happening to me. I was trying to find a logical answer since I was so faithful to God … how my life could now be in such shambles. *I even prayed during my sleep Lord! For what?* I thought.

"Why do all of that for you, and you desert me, ignore me, and not hear my cries? Why? You were my first love, I put no man before you! I just don't understand!" I said out loud.

Anger engulfed the very core of my soul. *I don't want to hear your name! I don't want to pray! I don't want to go to your house of worship! I don't want anything to do with you!*

I did everything God required of me. Why did He give me peace and then, allow it to escape from me so suddenly? Why did he allow Richard to torment me so? Hadn't I suffered enough already? I gave Richard the home and Jaden because of his threats and calculated manipulation. What else was there? There was nothing left.

Distraught and confused, searching for hope, any reason, why I should choose life? Richard, with all of his lies, had turned Jaden and my family against me. I demanded that my family choose Richard or either have nothing to do with me ever again!

"You should know me, why are you believing his lies?" I had asked my Grandmother Maxine. My grandmother was my best friend. I spoke to her at least five times a day.

"He's a good man Summer … what's wrong with you?" she asked. Angrily, I hung up the phone. I didn't care if she was still holding the receiver or not. I was livid. There was simply no reasoning with that woman any longer!

Believe whatever you want grandmother! Believe whatever you want! I thought. There was no hope for me. This insane man had convinced my entire family that *I* was walking away from a good marriage! It was my choice to make. We weren't living in the fifties anymore. Others in the family had divorced and others had not received this type of treatment. *Why was I being treated so differently?* I thought.

I tried to be the best wife I could by protecting him; by not allowing everyone to see his mishaps, trying to uplift him. No one can see the error of his ways. *Why, did I try to protect Richard?* I was so foolish. Richard had done nothing but scandalize my name in my own hometown after my departure.

How could my own family listen to his lies? Don't they know me? I am their blood! I've been a good Christian wife to this man for ten years, a great mother, a friend, lover, and everything in-between. I had so many thoughts going on in my head.

Do these people honestly believe I wanted to leave the only man I know and love? I have nothing, nothing at all. What is the point? Why am I even here? No one cares for me, no one! Why should I live? Everyone loves Richard so much. Well, you all can have Richard without me. Why should I live?* I wanted answers from God!

Forgiving my family was too hard of a pill to swallow for me at that point. Forgiving others (complete strangers) would have been much easier. That was a "no-brainer" for me. But, my family—no, my family on the other hand, had hurt me beyond repair by siding with Richard.

My family had known me since birth! Richard they only knew because of our marriage. Of course, they grew to love him as one of their own. Where on earth had they gotten the gall to entertain his lies and manipulation was completely beyond me!

"Summer, had been clubbing until the wee hours of the morning," He told family members. Or, that "I was dating a Jamaican drug dealer."

Really? I mean really family? It was beyond my comprehension how my intelligent family could entertain such foolishness.

I detested drug dealers. I would never have risked my life nor my freedom for drug money! Never, not ever! Sure people change, but I wasn't "people." I was their Summer; the quiet, well-mannered, Christian wife period!

I was loyal and faithful to my husband. I lowered my head in the mere presence of other men, certain not to give any false hope or for anything to ever be misconstrued. No eye contact was made–I never took that second look. There was no one who could take the place of Richard in my eyes. Shoot, I already had what most women wanted when they saw him.

How did I end up here? I wondered. An empty place … in a hollow marriage with no love left to give. I had become detached, separated before I ever even left him physically. Four years of begging, pleading, and asking Richard, "Please tell me what I am doing wrong?"

"You are doing nothing wrong Summer," He repeatedly said.

"I'm not happy Richard. I need you to change please baby, I love you!" I begged time and time again.

Yes, Summer you are understandably depleted. I thought. No refill. No refueling. No rejuvenating, no nothing! I was at rock bottom where my marriage was concerned. I had tried everything known to man. Did I love Richard? Absolutely! Was I in love with Richard at that point? Negative. The love had disintegrated. It had completely evaporated into thin air. At that point, I don't think the word "like" for Richard was even in my vocabulary.

A powerful woman of prayer is what my marriage had groomed me into becoming. I was no doubt a "praying wife." Morning ... yes, I prayed. Noon ... yes, and at night ... absolutely, yes I prayed! I was there constantly praying. It didn't seem to be enough, why?

In my eyes, it was as if Richard opened the front door and said to the devil, "Hello, there little red devil ... here is my beautiful family, feel free to have your way with them! I release them to you!"

My prayers were unanswered, but why? Maybe it had nothing to do with me, but more to do with God having to bring Mr. Richard down a notch or two. He had become so very arrogant in the ministry. Richard was at home constantly studying his sermons. However, he was at such a loss as to what was occurring in his very own household.

In Richard's eyes, and from what I heard him say, "There was no calling or anointing on Summer's life to do the work of the Lord in others." From his standpoint, Summer's position was only to be a submissive wife of a minister. The fact remained however, God in fact had used me to restore and rebuild countless marriages while in the midst of it all, mine was crumbling before my very eyes.

God had equipped us with everything we needed to be the "powerhouse" couple in ministry. Yet, how could we have been when my own husband was jealous of my works and the gifts God had given to me?

Richard had become too big to walk in his own shoes. Just the thought of uttering his name out of my mouth became unimaginable; Richard was an obnoxious and arrogant minister. Oh, he once was no doubt a bold soldier for the Lord; hands down, he could go toe to toe with the best of the best when it came to delivering and challenging the word of God.

But, God is a God of peace and He provides us abiding love. I saw neither in Richard anymore. I saw only vanity. Richard was playing with God Himself and this was a fight I was tip toeing backwards out of. I was not going to have any part of it.

I had gone down the street, around the corner, put it in reverse and went back around a second time before I realized I was in the same exact place ... absolutely, nowhere! I had two shadows; my husband and my son. I had absolutely zero outlets for myself.

I lost myself in the midst of ministering to others and saving souls. The last four years of my ten year marriage, melted as fast as marshmallows on an open flame; and the flame being the devil that Richard invited into our home. Where in the streets had Richard picked him up? That devil? I hadn't a clue.

The lustful spirits, the lies, the spirit of greed, Richard had become selfish and hungry for money like I had never witnessed before. This greed was overshadowing Richard's very existence. I always felt it was better "to give rather than to receive" and that had always been something Richard exercised so fervently as well ... well, up until now. But now, I no longer recognized him as the man I once loved. It was all about the the hard, cold, dirty cash money.

I had to take a step back from all of the emotions I was experiencing. I decided to take a moment to just walk around my very compact studio apartment. Although small, I cherished the still moments of peace in the air; the moments when Richard wasn't blowing up my phone. It was that day that I realized I was simply a trophy wife to Richard.

I saw that it wasn't about the ministry, our home, our son, our marriage, family, no, it was about Richard's pride, his big ego! It mattered to him how he looked in the eyes of others. It wasn't me that he missed. It was everything I represented, the "trophy wife." It was about the well-spoken, woman of class, pretty, petite wife who was always in her proper, respectful place ... on Richard's arm.

I thought back to a conversation that I once had with my daddy ....

"Richard controls you Summer!" Lex told me. "But, I do understand you wanting to be an obedient wife and play your role as his wife. You are doing right to stand by his side sweetheart," my daddy assured me. "But, he is controlling you babygirl nonetheless," he told me. If anyone knew, my daddy certainly knew what control was. Hell, his picture was next to the definition of "control" in the dictionary.

Even at a distance, Lex could discern it. I was limited to what I could say to my family and of course, to Richard's family. No one was listening to anything I had to say at that point, except my Lex. Richard didn't have him fooled by any means. I guess all of the others simply didn't give a damn enough about me.

If it weren't for my girlfriends from work, I really don't know how I could have survived it all. My girls kept me sane, they constantly kept me busy, and going and going.

Jaden was busy with his sports and Richard was busy brain washing him day by day. I just didn't have the energy to try to live and to fight with Richard. I waved the white flag up in the air, I surrendered all. *You've won Richard.* I thought. *You have everything I love most in this life, my son.*

He was slowly draining every ounce of life out of me.

"Summer, you are going to be fine!" Eboni told me.

"You're one of the strongest women I know girl," Zoe echoed.

"Yeah girl," Sasha chimed in.

"You won't let him take you down girl," they all said.

"Yeah," I mumbled.

Was I convinced of this myself at that time? Of course not; the motivation however, did encourage me some. Their support meant the world to me. It was their love, encouragement and support that gave me the inspiration to keep pushing forward. They all believed in me! I had to believe in myself, I just had to!!! My girlfriends solidified, all eyes were on me, Summer … watching, watching, and watching.

10

Amazing Graces

*O*ur friendship went far beyond the normal definition of friends. It was more of a sisterhood. There were seven of us, surely that guaranteed at least one of us would be available for another in a time of need. Whether that need was a listening ear, a spare bedroom, a meal, a financial loan, whatever the need, one of us was there to the rescue.

We were seven beautiful women; we had seven different personalities, backgrounds, cultures and all seven of us women were completely amazing.

My girlfriends were like family to me. We formed a special bond; it was like no other experience I had experienced before, with women. Of the seven, Eboni, Sasha and I were the ones who were absolutely inseparable. We were indeed, the female version of the "Three Musketeers." It wasn't very often you would see one without the other being somewhere in close proximity.

Instead of women fighting about designer labels, who is sleeping with who, and whatever the latest gossip was, we were immersing our lives with positive energy. The three of us went everywhere and I mean everywhere together; church services, trips, out dining, shopping, we even took care of one another's children.

At the time, little did we know that we were creating memories that would grieve our spirits for the rest of our lives.

Ring, ring, ring. "Hello," Eboni said.

"Hi sweetie, how's it going?" I asked.

"I'm good girl, how are you?" she replied.

"You know me, living my life as always," I said.

"Yes girl, that you do!" Eboni said.

"Listen Eboni, I never wanted things to get out of hand as bad as they did." I told her. "And for us to not speak for over a year was just foolish!" I continued. "It was just plain immature." I expressed.

"Yes, we both took things a little too far," she agreed. "Well, with experience and age comes life's lessons," she continued, "We've both grown and I know we can overcome any differences in the past."

"That's the key Eboni, it's the past," I replied.

"Of course you know I love you girl," Eboni said.

"And girl, I'll always love you," I told her. "Okay, that's enough with the mushy crap," I said.

In hindsight, looking back at our many arguments, they all seemed so foolish and petty. To lose a dear friend who was more like a sister was never a price either of us should've had to pay. Truthfully, Eboni and I knew we could never regain the lost years, but with maturity, we could possibly somehow establish a meaningful bond for a brighter future.

Years ago, Eboni and I both were women full of pride. We were both so full of feisty aggression. Yes, we were always too much alike for our own darn good. We were both born in the same birth month and we were a lot alike. I suppose the majority of our fights stemmed from us fighting for our own separate identities. Just as identical twins would, I suppose.

None of the other women fought or disagreed with one another for that matter. Nah, it was just Eboni and I. Fighting and arguing like two damn, wild alley cats! You name it and guaranteed, she and I had fought about it. We fought about men, we fought about parenting, we fought if the light was red and the other said it was green....

The harsh curse words hurt, they were like lashes across our hearts; as sharp as a belt buckle on a bare behind. We were vicious. I do mean vicious: v-i-c-i-o-u-s with our words! We didn't give a damn the damage the words would cause when they were released from our mouths.

Everyone felt the pain. The other ladies cringed when they witnessed the effects of our wrath! This was pain we managed to somehow camouflage for the rest of the ladies' sakes. No, they didn't deserve to be in the midst of our drag outs, no one did.

All fights aside, when it was time to head out for a night on the town, it was all fun times. I had to give it to Eboni, she was the one who cleaned up very nicely. She was a real head turner.

It was Eboni who hid her figure during the normal "nine to five." Nights on the town you'd swear she was a completely different woman. All other times, it was her casual attire she desired most; loose jeans, t-shirts, flip flops, wild hair and no makeup were her favored wardrobe choices.

Eboni, was from one of the most beautiful islands; her Caribbean accent intensified, without a doubt during a heated debate or argument. She had smooth, milk dark chocolate skin, a medium body frame and gorgeous, luxurious black hair.

Being a minister's wife, I had always been very respectful and I chose not to cause too much attention to my outer appearance. To be honest, I looked like an old, conservative married woman from the old days. In fact, it had actually been Eboni who convinced me to strip away my "church girl" image. Instead, she said I would be more appealing if I'd show off more of my athletic, petite figure which had been a feature of mine that was envied by most.

There was no life, no zest, and no rays of sunshine in me then! Although, some may beg to differ. Reality was, I didn't see it in myself. That's what mattered most, right? I felt as though I was dying a slow death every single day.

At the time, I looked, I felt, and I lived every bit of someone well beyond the ripe age of thirty. How was that possible, when I hadn't drank or smoked as many of my peers had? Well, I realized I didn't have to do those things because I later learned what the smoke, alcohol and drugs didn't do, unhappiness and stress would do on its own.

Having married so young, I never had a social life with real girlfriends while I was growing up. It was work, church, home and family trips. My life was consumed with family, close friends and church. I never had any outside activities or other outlets for venting accessible to me.

And then came along Eboni, I thanked God for her! There she was, a woman who taught me how to let my hair down and run free.

When Eboni and I met, neither of us knew exactly how much we would become indebted to one another. She had moved to Florida from Jersey City, not knowing a soul. It almost appeared as though she had been running from something or someone. When I met her, it was very apparent her spirit was haunted by a dark past. In fact, the first time I laid eyes on Eboni, I knew her spirit was broken. Her heart was so very heavy; I remember her being in so much pain, I could feel her pain the moment we embraced each other. Our pain identified with each other's pain instantly. It was clear Eboni was in need of genuine love and I couldn't have been placed in her life at a more opportune time for her.

My spirit was a very discerning one back then. It never deceived me nor led me wrong, ever! Little did either of us know that I too, would soon also need her just as much as she needed me. Time later revealed that I would actually need all six of my girlfriends, but each one at completely separate times and for different reasons.

Looking down at the text on my phone, it read:

"Nothing is like it used to be anymore, my life isn't the same! I miss what we all once shared. We all were so close, especially us Summer." Zoe texted.

"I know, but I can no longer be the one keeping the strings tied together Zoe. I'm tired Zoe, it's time to pass

the torch. I'm sorry, these shoes are too big for me to fill." I wrote back.

"I know, I know.   I'm going to send an email to everyone, it's been years and we need to plan an "Amazing Graces" reunion," Zoe wrote. Although Zoe's intentions were good, I had serious doubts that our relationships could or would ever be restored to their original states.

We all had grown into different people now. We were in different places; in different circumstances and we had different visions, lives, not to mention different area codes. I wouldn't dare discourage Zoe though. She reminded me of the kind and sweet natured side of my personality.

Each of the women represented something completely different from the other. Zoe, was the easy going, spiritual, peaceful, and warm personality of the seven women. There were a few occasions where Zoe would make me raise an eyebrow or two when her freaky side escaped; it wasn't so much of the things she did though, but more of the things she said.

Zoe hadn't fooled me for one second. I knew she was straight up "knocking the boots" off of her husband, Anthony. Zoe was my girl; she confided in me, and you best believe her secrets would always remain safe.

Zoe was British. And boy, did she ever bring her diversity, style, and culture to the forefront! She was tall, almost six feet and all legs like that of a top model. Her skin appeared kissed, caramel kisses from the sun. Her humor was surprising and at the strangest times ... and oh man, did she love her calypso and soca music! With the sound of each beat, Zoe could "whine" her lil' hips along with the rhythms; she seemed to always escape into those erotic sounds.

With all sincerity I tried my best to encourage Zoe. "Sweetie, I feel your pain, we all feel it at times." I told her. "But ...." I paused I didn't want to kill her hope of excitement for our reunion. So instead, I did like any good girlfriend would, I gave Zoe the possibility of hope. "... Give it a try Zoe, maybe this time it will work." I replied. Truth be told, most of us would probably have done whatever it took to make it happen, except Amber and Madison.

Amber's, Zoe's, and Gabrielle's passports all had fresh ink stamped in them. Madison was more laid back; she on the other hand, had two small children at home, yet, you best believe Madison found time for her girls. She always believed in letting her hair down though.

Although, Madison had two adorable small children, she was a glowing beauty. Her dimples were deeply impressed within her cheeks; you could place your fingers in them. Her teeth were sparkling white. Her skin was flawless. There was no need for any makeup where Madison was concerned. She was one radiant beauty; long legs, tall and a small frame would best describe this beauty. Motherhood was very kind to Madison. She was a native Floridian. There were always men surrounding her anytime we went out; her smile would melt them like butter every time, it was sure to lure them right in.

I can honestly say there was not one single time that Madison and I ever disagreed, nor had an argument; nothing, not a one. Rare, yes, but we never, ever did! Anytime I wanted to listen to some live music, or get my two-step on, I could count on Madison to be my escort.

"Pretty forehead" was what one intoxicated man referred to her as. Why this man was infatuated with her forehead was beyond any of us. Perhaps it was the one too many drinks that was the true culprit.

Amber, Amber, Amber. Amber was in a class of her own; she was of Irish persuasion and her complexion was a few shades lighter than any of ours. None of us saw color though, Amber was our sister, period. Shoot, Amber had more spice in her than any of us African American sistahs. Amber's long, blonde hair in our group pictures was quite the visual reminder that we came from different backgrounds and cultures.

Amber was a smart, witty, sharp and fiery lil' lady and she was always the voice of reason of the seven of us. At the same time, she was unwed and had her mind focused on obtaining her master's degree. Education was the priority for her.

Amber, Gabrielle and I once resided in the same gated apartment community. It was a luxury apartment community predominately of young business professionals. This is where Gabrielle and I had initially met. All of the others and I had met at work.

Gabrielle and I were both at the leasing office, patiently awaiting assistance. I had been there checking on reserving a space to have a small "get-together." I was always planning some form of entertainment by the pool and Jacuzzi or in my studio apartment. A studio was all I could afford in that expensive community. I still had significant jointly-held financial obligations with Richard which meant my funds were extremely low. But, I wasn't by any means willing to sacrifice the lifestyle I was accustomed to.

Immediately, I noticed Gabrielle. She was what blacks refer to as "thick." In most men's eyes, "thick" was a very, very good thing. She had runner's legs; perhaps some would describe her shape as that of tennis player's.

Gabrielle was a Nubian African princess, she was from Ghana. Her facial features confirmed it; they were very distinguished. Her nose, sharp; her lips, full. Her smile, wide; and her teeth, pearly white. Her skin was flawless. She was simply beautiful.

Gabrielle had moved to Florida from north Philly. She knew absolutely no one when she arrived. She had received a job offer as a registered nurse in our area. At twenty-three, Gabrielle was much younger than the rest of us. Amber was the oldest, next was Eboni, then myself, Madison, Sasha and lastly Gabrielle, in that order.

Gabby, (short for Gabrielle) had her "I's dotted" and her "T's crossed. Well, all except for in the "Men's Department." Hell, what am I saying? *None* of us were successful in that department! Maybe, just maybe, a few of us had a slight clue....

Having a career and being pretty wasn't quite working out as Gabrielle had hoped. The doctors weren't looking to do anything except "play doctor" with her if you know what I mean. Gabrielle on the other hand was looking for something more along the lines of a commitment, so, their advances were just not acceptable.

She was eager to establish a solid, long-term relationship with a family-oriented young man.

I, being the friendly, "people person" that I was, I immediately welcomed her into our cozy yet, unfamiliar community. On that particular day, the rest of the girls and I were at the poolside, simply enjoying a nice sunny Florida day.

Gabrielle's "vibe" was a positive one from my first impression of her, so I felt comfortable extending an invitation for her to join us.

"Sure, I would love to come," she said.

"Great, we'll see you around four or so," I replied.

Sasha seemed to take mostly to Gabrielle initially, probably because of their mad obsession for shoes! They both had a serious collection of name brand shoes.

I met Sasha through an interview process at work. She interviewed for a position in our marketing department where Madison and I already worked; we were responsible for the advertising. Amber and Eboni were both in separate departments; they handled the customer relations. Zoe handled stock portfolios in yet another department.

Sasha was already a respected employee of the company. However, she was simply seeking opportunity for growth. Sasha, of course nailed the interview. She was poised, "calm, cool and collected." It was a unanimous decision and we were elated to have Sasha become a part of our team.

After a few weeks of feeling Sasha out, I learned that she was a single mother of a beautiful young daughter. She was also attending college in order to obtain her second degree in Business. Sasha had class, finesse and an attitude with sass. Her wardrobe and northern Chicago flavor didn't hurt either. You could definitely see the Native American blood in her features, hair and beautiful complexion. I thought she'd be a great addition to our sisterhood. She'd also be someone that I could put Eboni off on when I didn't have the energy to run across the city with her shopping!

The majority of Sasha's family were back up north. She only had her brother here and a few other relatives. Yeah, Sasha fit into our equation perfectly. We were all professional women with benefits, stock options, and growth potential. But, our love lives were a completely different story, they sucked!

My girlfriends were great! They were almost everything that I needed at the time ... they filled my life with such an array of diversity. With all of the love and attention they all brought, there was still something missing though. And that something was a someone! I would soon discover that someone's name would be Ray.

The Most Loved

11

Forgive Us Father

$\mathcal{R}$ ay called and asked me to forgive him. Truth be told, I had forgiven Ray a long, long time ago. I don't think it had anything at all to do with his orders to go overseas. Or had it? No, honestly, it was my belief that it had everything to do with him knowing deep within in his heart that it was simply the right thing to do.

Ray needed to beg for my forgiveness. He needed to apologize. He needed to say that he was sorry. Sorry, for the horrific way he treated me. It was undeserved. He had been called "an utterly damn fool!" by my girlfriends.

Me forgiving Ray wasn't for him, it was for me! I needed it far more than Ray. I needed to forgive myself that I ever allowed anyone to make me feel such self-loath. I was worthy of being loved. I could be appreciated and cared for—I could absolutely live a life of happiness and I knew it! When I forgave myself, I gained all of that and then some!

In hindsight—looking back at Ray and my humble beginning, who was really to blame? The military lifestyle he led was not something that was unfamiliar to me; I knew exactly what it entailed.

MacDill Air Force Base was practically at my front door. The condo community where I lived was saturated with military personnel. In fact, some of those soldiers were very dear friends of mine.

A soldier's lifestyle brought no fear to me. I wasn't intimidated by the military lifestyle in the least. I saw firsthand, what war had done to my daddy mentally. The mental residues of war presented a social challenge to many veterans; it was a challenge for many of them to just live a normal, everyday life as a civilian.

The battles of war continued in their minds every single day. Things civilians took for granted, soldiers had a completely different perspective on. From my standpoint, they had more of an appreciation for life than others did who had not been to war.

Things we considered an obstacle were really not obstacles for them at all; our problems, were really not serious problems through their eyes. They ate, slept, and breathed the possibility of going to war every day. Their lives were under the control of a man known to civilians as "Uncle Sam."

12

Fools Rush In

"You may want to slow down Ray," Sasha said. "I think you really should take your time with Summer. Have fun, enjoy one another's company.

"She's my world," He told her.

Sasha knew I would feel like a frightened rabbit trapped in a corner and that I would run at the first opportunity if someone threw the word "commitment" or "relationship" at me!

Ray stared up at Sasha with those gorgeous hazel eyes of his and said "Yeah, yeah."

But, Sasha cautioning Ray, was indeed, the best advice she ever could have given to him. It's just too bad that Ray didn't take heed. Ray wanted what he wanted and that was "me" Summer!

Ray was a very smart man, he was quite aware that Sasha and I would later talk about their conversation. You can bet that's exactly what happened!

"Personally, I too think it's just a little too soon for Ray to be feeling such strong feelings for you Summer," Sasha cautioned me. "He's only known you a little over a month."

"Yes, and you know me girl, I am not one to jump into something so fast," I assured her. My mind was far removed from any type of commitment. I had become a playgirl—one of the finest! Having been with only one man for fifteen years, I wanted to explore. I wanted to live life and have some fun!

"Girl, you have your hands full with that one!" She said. "You better be very careful," Sasha warned.

"Girl, you know me. I got this!" I bragged.

I had everything under control with Ray. I thought, *I will just keep him at bay because he was stationed out of the state.*

"What are you going to do?" Sasha asked.

"Well, I'm just going to sit Ray down and have a conversation with him," I told her.

I tried very hard to convince myself that Ray would understand. I was eager to just sit Ray down and tell him exactly how I felt. I practiced several approaches with myself in the mirror:

"Look Ray, I think you are a great guy and I really am very fond of you I would like to see where this could lead down the road, but now is just too soon for me I'm still trying to get a divorce from my husband. I don't want to bring all of this baggage into a new relationship." I practiced saying, over and over.

Looking in the mirror, as I spoke those words aloud to myself, I felt that Ray should completely understand. I was nervous all the same, but I thought; *He'll understand. He'll be fine*. I concluded.

I shook my head knowing wholeheartedly that it just wasn't going to fly, at least not at that point in time. No way was Ray ready to receive or accept my professions of freedom. Perhaps, months down the road–perhaps my heart would change. I finally decided that particular conversation with Ray wasn't a battle I was ready to armor myself up to fighting at that time.

The Most Loved

13

The Glamorous Life

$\mathcal{I}$ had always been afraid to fly in an airplane. Richard and I always drove to our destinations because of my fear of flying.

I would always say, "At least I can control anything that happens on the ground, but, I know I have no control in the air!"

"I'm sending you a ticket to fly up to North Carolina to visit me," Ray said. He was a sergeant first class in the Army. He was stationed at Fort Bragg, North Carolina.

"Wow, look at the clouds," I said to myself as I looked out of the window. *This is what I've been missing all this time? Shame on me*. I thought.

I was in such a state of awe. "This is simply breathtaking," I said. *Look at the clouds, so fluffy and transparent!* I felt so close to God at that moment. I felt so free. I felt I had finally found who Summer was at that very moment and I found out what living truly was!

Were those angels within those clouds? Or, maybe angels were flying alongside the plane at that very moment. I thought.

"Wow, is this really what it's all about Lord?" I said out loud. I took a quick peek around to make sure no one saw me talking to myself. I didn't care though, I was as free as a bird!

I inhaled, exhaled and then, sighed as I fell back into my seat. Ray had purchased me an mp3 player during his last visit to Florida. He wanted to make sure I had my music whenever I exercised. I reached into my book bag, pulled out my headphones, and got lost in the sounds of soulful music. That is where I escaped.

I danced in my seat until I exhausted myself. I knew the other passengers thought I was a bit "loco" a few times. I glanced over and smiled at a few of them. Hell, I was happy and I wanted to shout it to the world! Who cared what those perfect strangers thought? Well, I most certainly didn't care at all because "I was living my life," I sang.

What a smooth plane ride it had been. I was so upset at myself. What was all the fuss about? There was really nothing to the airplane ride. There had been absolutely no turbulence, something that I heard others complain about when they traveled. It was simply a nice, smooth, mellow flight on a beautiful Friday evening.

"It is now 78 degrees," the pilot announced as we approached the airport for landing. All I could see below us were tiny lights everywhere. It was an amazing sight to see!

Yeah, this here was living! It had been years since I had been to North Carolina and it was the very first time I had been to Fort Bragg. I wasn't sure what to expect knowing it was a military base. It had been my first trip invading Ray's space, "his territory" one would say. I just looked out of the window in total silence. I was uncertain of what to expect or what to do next so, I simply followed the crowd.

"Honey, I'm here … I've landed," I said.

"Ok babe, I'm parking the truck. I'll be right there," He said. Ray immediately spotted me. He lifted me off my feet as he kissed me all over and hugged me. "I'm so happy to see you baby. I've missed you," He said.

"I've missed you too babe," I said.

Ray had the most gorgeous hazel eyes and the longest eyelashes. I always seemed to get lost inside his eyes anytime he would look at me. His crooked smile was simply beautiful and his teeth were bright white. We won't even mention his minty fresh breath! Ray's warm, beautiful smile always reassured me of his love for me each time we met.

"Thanks for sending for me babe," I said gratefully. It felt good to finally see his neck of the woods. Even if I had absolutely no idea what was awaiting me.

Ray and I began to walk, but as we walked he abruptly stopped dead in his tracks.

"Hold on a minute baby!" He said. There was a soldier there in the airport who was not dressed appropriately. Ray tore him apart right there in front of everyone. I wasn't sure if all of that was necessary, but I was embarrassed for everyone involved. I was embarrassed for the soldier, and for Ray, for having felt the need to reprimand him publicly. I was embarrassed for me too, because of the stares of disgust that fell upon all three of us from people passing by.

Ray walked back over to me. "Baby, I'm really sorry I should not have done that," he said. He realized that instead, he should have pulled the soldier aside. "I went a little overboard," he said.

Who knew exactly? Perhaps, Ray was trying to impress me with his authority. Either way, it was embarrassing. I was so embarrassed. We all were.

Ray grabbed me by my hand as we walked through the airport to his truck. He was always a gentleman, so he politely opened the truck door, and helped me up into my seat.

As I climbed up into the truck, there lied a red, single, long stemmed rose on the seat. Ray never ceased to amaze me! His generosity was overwhelming at times. Ray spoiled me so much that my mommy advised him that he should stop showering me with too many gifts. Ray had the ability to make me feel like a princess. He made me feel like the world was mine for the taking!

Money was never an issue when it came to Ray and me. He was accustomed to quality things and so was I. I never expected anything from him. Additionally, everyone knew that I was always provided the best things in life from my family and from my ex-husband. It wasn't like it was some big secret. The fact of the matter, from the moment Ray saw my residence for the first time, he knew that I had attained a high standard of living.

Ray had a thing for watches. He was addicted to them. He made certain that I had watches too. He wanted to ensure that I changed watches throughout the week. "Guess" designer watches were his favorite; they had that prissy, "princess" look that Ray desired to see me rock. Kenneth Cole was also one of Ray's favorite designers. He owned Kenneth Cole everything; shoes, shorts, pants, belts, cologne, cufflinks, sun glasses, watches, and wallets. If Kenneth Cole made it, you best believe Ray owned it! Ray always had the best of the best....

I walked into Ray's room. It reminded me of a dorm room however, it was very spacious. Ray said that his room was a little larger than the others due to his rank. He lived on base which saved him money from having to pay room and board elsewhere each month. I suppose Ray thought this gave him a right to blow money away, as though he owned the ink and paper in which it was printed on.

His room was comfortable quarters. It had a separate living room, a bathroom, and an area with a sink and microwave. He led me towards the back where his sleeping quarters were. He had a twin bed, television, laptop, and his clothes in that area. An alarm should have sounded in my head when I discovered Ray had already purchased toiletries for me.

"Hey babe, I bought some soap for your face that I want you to use," he said.

I had always had flawless skin. I never had a need to wear makeup at all, but, since the divorce ordeal, the stress had caused major acne to break out on my face and back. My dermatologist advised me to simply wash my face with either Ivory or Dove soap and avoid using all of the over the counter cleansing products. Ray had purchased Dove "sensitive skin" soap for me, a tooth brush, and whatever other toiletries that were sold in the stores. He always knew exactly what I needed and what was best for me.

Somehow the entire setting had started to remind me of a hospital; it reminded me of an ill person in need of assistant living.

"Here sit your things down," he said. "Let me warn you, the bugle will sound at 5 a.m. for P.T.," he said. Ray explained that "P.T." was "personal training" when soldiers had to get up for their morning run if they were on duty that day. Sure enough, I jumped straight up in the bed when the horn sounded at 5 a.m. on the dot! I looked around in a panic, only to realize it was just the P.T. horn.

Ray had to step out for a few so I lied in bed unable to fall back asleep. I was in an unfamiliar place. My mind began to drift back to a few trips we shared while Ray was in Florida visiting with me. We had gone to International Plaza in Tampa Bay, the "Baller and Shot Callers" mall!

At International Plaza you could find: valet parking for the fancy cars, divas dressed to impress in their stilettos, fine dining, and clubs for the professionals, and top designer stores (Tiffany, Movado, Gucci etc.) It was like a scene taken from "Lifestyles of The Rich and Famous."

"Man, babe, this is really nice," Ray said. He was amazed at how exotic the path to the entrance to the mall was. We finally made our way inside the actual mall to head over to Dillard's department store. "Look around to see if there's anything you like in here babe," Ray just shooed me away!

About thirty minutes later. "Honey, I've found some great deals," I smiled as I pulled Ray over to the junior's section.

"Ok, give me a fashion show... let's see the jeans on first," Ray said as he winked. I must have modeled eight pairs of jeans along with eight tops for him.

A few hours later, and completely exhausted, he said, "Ok, you've worn me out. Now, get what you want babe and let's go." I picked through several pairs of jeans and tops and proceeded to the counter. Ray turned around with a look of confusion.

"Where are all the things you tried on?" he asked.

"I put them back honey!" I said.

"Girl, if you don't go over there and get those clothes! Baby, I'm getting all of them for you!" Ray told me.

Tears filled my eyes. "Wow babe, are you serious? All of this for me?" I asked.

"Of course babe," Ray smiled. It wasn't the fact that I wasn't accustomed to being spoiled. I've always had everything I wanted growing up as a child. Even as a wife, I never wanted for anything from Richard. That time was different. That time it was *very* different! Ray wasn't my husband, or my parents, or grandparents, aunts or uncles. In fact, legally, I was technically still Richard's wife. Ray was someone new.

"You'll never find another man like me!" Richard told me. *Well Richard, you are wrong because someone has found me who is indeed better.* I thought with excitement!

The Most Loved

14

Guess Who's For Dinner?

"Summer, Summer" Ray called. "Girl, where were you? In the twilight zone?" he asked. He had a puzzled look on his face.

"I called you at least five times already! Are you ready to go eat breakfast? Then, I can show you around the base." he said.

"Sure, baby let's go!" I said. I was excited to be leaving his quarters.

I felt eye balls scanning me from head to toe as we made our way around base. Ray was very careful to only introduce me to a few people. And by the smiles of those two, I could tell Ray was ready to get me as far away from the base as he could!

Of course, there were plenty of men there on base, but I considered myself to have one of the top notch guys so why would I even waste my time looking?

Ray made sure to give me the most important rules so that I wouldn't break any while I was visiting him.

The most important rule for me, because Ray knew I had a led foot, was to respect the base speed limit.

"Do not mess around Summer with your heavy foot here on base," Ray warned.

"I will respect the law Ray," I assured him.

We prepared to head to Raleigh to visit my family; Raleigh was less than an hour away. My cousins who lived there were always giving me a hard time; they complained that I never wanted to leave Florida to visit anywhere else.

The truth of the matter, I lived in "paradise" so why should I have wanted to leave? However, reality was, there was an entire world out there that I hadn't even tapped the surface of. I had not been to Raleigh in years, since I was a child actually. And now, Ray was getting an opportunity to meet my family. How privileged Ray was!

A storm blew me in the day Ray and I drove up. Well not literally, but it took a "leap of faith" to finally get me there! A leap of faith, a pending divorce, and a generous man who loved me enough to make it all possible. My Aunt Renee, and her two daughters Traci and Brittany, lived in Raleigh.

My family was known for their warm affection and for being loads of fun. We all were a loud group of family members! I don't know if it was something in our genetic make-up where our hearing was impaired or what, but we all talked loud, as though we were deaf! No one seemed to be excused from loud talking in our family; my mommy, her mom, her sister, her sister's daughters, all loud—loud talking women!

My mommy's younger sister Renee, she didn't look her age. She was petite and gorgeous. Just as gorgeous as the rest of the women in our family all were. We always joked that I was more like my Aunt Renee and that my aunts' daughters were more like my mommy.

When Ray and I arrived, they all ran out of the garage straight to the vehicle welcoming us with hugs and kisses.

"Girl, you are looking more like your mom by the day," my Aunt Renee said. It was amazing—our family resemblance. There was definitely no mistake that we were what southerners called "kin folk." Oh and Ray, he fit right in with the family. Yes, he was a tad bit shy at first. After an incident with my Aunt Renee, he was officially declared part of the family.

Yep, yes she did … my aunt grabbed Ray on his behind! If that wasn't bad enough, she only did it to call my mommy to tell her that he had a nice butt! It appeared to be exactly what Ray needed to warm up.

Any man that couldn't fit into my family's sense of humor and affectionate ways definitely wouldn't be a good fit for me either. My aunt was harmless. She was simply having fun with us all and trying to get Ray to warm up. Especially, since all of them had grilled him with a zillion questions about his intentions with me over dinner at the seafood restaurant.

The "butt grab" was a welcomed change for Ray I'm sure! He and my Aunt Renee were best buddies after that. We couldn't get Ray to shut up once he became alive. It didn't help either, that my aunt bragged to my mommy about how handsome Ray was with his gorgeous eyes and nice body. Did I get upset? Not at all, it was family! We laughed, we joked, we had fun and we enjoyed one another's company. In fact, so much so that when we got back to the house, we played some board games and we sipped on some wine.

Please tell me how one bottle of wine could turn into my cousin Brittany having to make a run to the store for more bottles. It was a dessert wine that simply left your mouth wet. It had the appearance of innocence, but once opened, it was naughty. It put you on your behind completely wasted!

After our tipsiness wore off, it was time to head back to the base. Leaving my family was hard. It had been so long since I had been Raleigh. Ray and I were both tired on the ride back. Thank God the ride was a short one!

15

You Lost A Good Thing

Trips were becoming the norm for Ray and me. He would call me in advance to be on the lookout for incoming mail which always included the itinerary for our next rendezvous.

The most memorable of all of our trips was the one we made to Saint Augustine, Florida. It was such a small town, but so romantic. It was full of history, culture and of course, the ocean!

The famous Ray Charles received his education from the school for the deaf and the blind in Saint Augustine. The "Fountain of Youth," along with tales of haunted houses and "The Fort" were all tourist sites. Not to mention many more historical landmarks such as "The Old Jail."

You better believe we took lots and lots of pictures. We were happy then! Sure, we had our normal arguments you have when you are getting to know one another. Some call it "growing pains." I called it "simply love."

"Simply love" is when you care enough to want a resolution so you can both move forward in the relationship. You ask questions, argue and openly communicate because you are attempting to reach an understanding....

When the arguments cease, and when the questions no longer form ... you've lost "simply love." No one cares enough anymore to want to do anything at all. The love is no longer "simple." It's what society calls "complicated."

Well, Ray and I were in our "simply love" stage ... we were still caring enough to want to move forward. And with all of the elaborate gifts and fun filled trips, one would think we were already an item.

Truth of the matter, we did everything together, but it was not enough for me to want to commit to Ray. I had begun seeing the signs, one I saw in my daddy that I was all too familiar with.

Yes, the control was becoming more evident! I saw the possibility of potential abuse. It became more frightening with each passing week. Abuse, it was very possible with Ray. I slowly became afraid; I was thinking of the possibility of being moved far, far away from my family. Around that same time, Ray was growing tired of waiting on me to fall in line with his aspirations and plans for our future.

I wanted to slowly start putting a little distance between us, to at least attempt getting some space. But, I didn't know how to at that point. I had allowed Ray too much control over the situation already. No, he wasn't hearing it neither was he trying to have it at all!

But, I did have control! I had been unknowingly controlled my entire life ... by my parents, especially my daddy! And, not to mention—my soon to be ex-husband. Everyone was claiming they wanted to protect me! From what? Myself? I had the control over what would happen in the next chapter of my life! I finally had freedom!

Who was everyone trying to protect me from ... was it the world? Was it men? Was it life itself? What the hell was it that everyone was trying to protect me from that I was too damn blind to see for myself? Could someone please let me, Summer in on the big secret? I was becoming angry. Angry that Ray loved me way too damn much! Just as my parents had, just as Richard had, hell as everyone had!

Why was I "most loved?" The attention, the admiration was always sure to follow everywhere I went. It was a glow which protruded from within me outward that people gravitated to and became fixed upon. *My*

*goodness, it was no fault of my own, take it up with the
Lord,* I thought. *God made me beautiful; just as He
makes everything beautiful.* I was convinced.

Placed on a pedestal by every man I encountered, if
I had placed myself on this pedestal perhaps, just
perhaps ... I could understand. But, I had not. *So, why
had they?* I wondered.

I dated casually during my separation from Richard.
Meeting men came easily. The girls and I were always
going someplace. And coming easily, Dominic was one
who fit right into that equation almost instantly. He had
moved here from "Chi-town." He opened my mind to
new horizons. I was slowly introduced to the various
essences of wine tasting through him. The differences
between red and white; which wine was suited best for a
particular meal....

Dominic explored my musical depth; we approached
jazz with a newfound appreciation that I had yet to
discover. And there was "Soul Food" I knew it all too
well, however, preparing cuisine at home was unfamiliar
territory that I would soon become very familiar with
through Dominic's education.

I could let my hair down with Dominic. He was a free
spirit. We laughed. We talked. We shared. Dominic was
a friend first before anything became romantic between us.

He taught me how to explore my sexuality. He was patient, extremely patient. I was a frightened kitten in the bedroom and he was the warm home which provided fresh milk. His patience ultimately led to perfection in the bedroom. My eagerness to learn only excited Dominic to teach more … I discovered what it truly meant to please a man thanks to him.

Love making is a form of art. Our bodies are canvases upon which to paint a rainbow of colors, shapes, and contrasts and Dominic made a magnificent masterpiece when he instructed me, "his student" in "the art of love making." We reached elevations which caused my legs to shake as uncontrollable seizures. His pleasures satisfied me in such a way; the next day, I was still feeling the warmth of his sensations.

Unfortunately, in due time Dominic was like everyone else in my life. He wanted me all to himself; he was no different. Although, not immediately … he too, sadly became controlling.

And just like Dominic, Ray was no exception either. It was the same type of love I had seen my entire life … that "crazy love!" I wasn't ready to be loved so deeply, so soon. Richard hadn't come to terms with our pending divorce. After just casually dating … why would I want to repeat the same vicious cycle all over again? Marriage? No sir, I wasn't ready!

Did I have love for Ray? Absolutely! I loved the man he was. I knew his intentions were good. I knew in his heart the love he had for me was real. I knew he didn't want to hurt me. But, another marriage so soon would have been completely insane! Jumping out of one marriage right into another ... I vowed that I would never marry again once I was free from Richard. Marriage was not going to be in my cards I promised myself.

So, how was it I found myself in that predicament with Ray? I was so upset with myself for allowing it to happen so soon. No, it wasn't going down like that! Once Ray had returned home from our trip, I finally found enough courage to bring the subject up in conversation. It was time we discussed the matters of *my* heart.

"Ray, honey, we need to talk," I told him.

"About?" He asked.

"Us," I replied.

"I'm listening," he said.

"Babe, you know that I love you right?" I asked.

"Yeah babe," he said. His tone was very quiet. "Well, with my divorce not yet final and Richard continuing to contest it by purposely not filing papers ordered, this divorce is taking forever," I said.

"Summer, this isn't about your damn divorce," Ray said. "You know f—king well that this isn't so don't you go trying to play me like it is!" Don't play with my intelligence Summer, don't you dare go giving me this b—llshit!" He said.

I paused before I responded. I knew everything he said was indeed true. It really didn't have anything to do with my divorce. It should have, but it didn't! It had taken me thirty years to finally have the freedom to make my own decisions and I wasn't going to give that up so freely this time around!

Yes, Ray had wine and dined me for six months with trips and gifts and more. It was never about the gifts, trips and financial tokens of love. Ray was getting something in return as well, me! I was giving Ray my affection, my attention, my time. Ray was receiving his own share of pleasure in return.

I had asked Ray some time ago to stop with the lavish gifts and to instead, save his money. He didn't need to impress or try to buy me. I was convinced of Ray's love. He had surely proven himself.

I had gone away for the weekend to clear my head. One of my friends from Vegas had flown down and invited me to hangout. Boy, what a big mistake! I knew Perry had a thing for me true enough, but I didn't realize the extent of his intentions. Perry and I had met through a mutual acquaintance.

He was an aspiring author. What an incredible talent he had that I simply admired. He had mailed me the transcript of his first book to get my honest opinion. Can you say "amazing?" I must have gone through a minor depression after I was done reading it. I felt the characters had been a part of my daily life for weeks. I had become Perry's biggest fan! I felt his book was surely "best seller" bound.

Through Perry's and my mutual love for writing, we began to talk more on the phone. At some point I began to see Perry's feelings towards me grow into something more on a romantic level. Nonetheless, I accepted the invitation. Why I accepted the invitation, I wasn't quite sure. I suppose it was a test for me; a test to see if I was truly in love with Ray.

The entire time I was with Perry, all I could do was think about Ray. I wished for Perry to be gone and Ray to be there instead. There was no romantic interest there for me at all. Why had I gone there? From the moment I arrived, in the same step, I wanted to turn my feet right around and leave. I didn't want to be there.

"Why are you crying?" My mommy asked. "Summer, what's wrong? You are scaring me," She said.

"I'm sorry mommy, I'm ok," I said.

"You don't sound ok Summer," She said.

"Ray called me and said he can't do this anymore!" I told her. "Ray said after six months I should know what I want."

"Summer, I'll have to agree with Ray" she said. "Are you not in love with Ray, Summer?" she asked.

"Yes, I love him mommy," I replied.

"What's the problem?" She asked.

"I'm afraid mommy," I said.

There was a separate room for the toilet inside of the bathroom where I was hiding from Perry. He had given me the master bedroom to sleep in, but the walls were thin. Perry had gone all out with the resort reservation. We were staying at a nice resort in Miami. It had a jacuzzi in the master bedroom that could seat three comfortably.

I thought the weekend was just what I needed. Boy, was I wrong! I didn't want to risk Perry overhearing my conversation with my mommy. I cared enough for him to not want to hurt him. He was a good man, just not the man that I loved.

My tears were uncontrollable at that moment. Perry had fallen asleep, or so I thought, on the couch. He had made himself a nice pad on the leather sleeper sofa. My cries were hard to ignore even through the door.

"Summer sweetheart, what's wrong?" Perry asked. *Knock, knock.* Perry knocked on the door to make sure I was okay. "Did I do something dear?" He asked.

My cries had become more intense. I went into the bathroom and turned the shower on. I forced myself into the warm water. I cried so much until I found myself outside of my own body. I had begun speaking in an "unknown tongue." At that moment, surely only God understood what I was saying to Him. I never had the gift to interpret "unknown tongues" only the gift to speak it.

All I knew at that moment was that there had only been one other time I experienced speaking in tongues since leaving Richard.

God had answered my cries! I thought. He showed me exactly where my heart lied. I had no business being there in Miami. My place was with Ray and I knew it at that point. But, I didn't know how I could fix it at that point.

I reached for my car keys as I ran out the door explaining to Perry that I needed some fresh air. The door immediately slammed behind me. I couldn't reach the vehicle fast enough to call Ray. But, I knew better than to call him immediately. I knew Perry well enough to know that he would soon be down to ensure that I wasn't racing off in my car. Bless his heart, poor thing didn't know what to think or do. Perry was completely dumbfounded.

"Summer, why now?" Ray asked. "You are only saying you want to be with me now out of fear. People on my job are asking what is wrong with me," he continued. "I'm walking around like a zombie! This is what your love has done to me Summer."

I begged Ray from deep within my soul to please let me prove to him that I was ready for a commitment.

"I can't do it Summer," he said. I cried and begged Ray until there was nothing left in me. "Bye Summer," Ray said. Ray hung up the phone and I hung my head.

After realizing Ray was the man I was in love with and now I've lost him, I just sat in my car, numb! I couldn't move, I couldn't think. I couldn't do anything!

The Most Loved

16

First Impressions

"*I* love you Summer," Ray said. "I can't do this without you baby.

"I love you too. I thought I had lost you," I said.

"You had," He replied. "You must have done some serious praying to baby Jesus!"

If only you knew how much. I wanted to tell him. "Let's just say God answers prayers. What now?" I asked.

I was all the way in with Ray now. I made up my mind that I was throwing in my "player's card." Ray had become "my ace." We could "always count on one another every time" we promised.

More trips were planned. More visits were made. An entire year had already gone by so fast. Ray and I committed to seeing one another every other weekend. Either I was flying there, or Ray was coming to Florida. More often, Ray was coming to Florida. After all, who wouldn't want to come to "sunny Florida?"

Time began to pass and things began becoming pretty serious between Ray and me. We both felt it was time that I finally met his family. Ray was the only boy. He had two sisters, Tonya and Layla.

There had always been doubt in Ray's mind that the man who had raised him and his two sisters wasn't his biological father. It was always like having salt poured into an open wound whenever Ray would visit his hometown in Tennessee.

Ray pleaded time and time again for the answers from his mom. Yet, she never would admit to Ray the truth. Ray had told me there was a man in their small town, who he looked exactly identical to.

Ray had a red skin tone, hazel eyes, and a nice small frame. The Native American Indian in his bloodline was very apparent just as it was in my own features and skin tone. I could immediately see the Indian and Caucasian in his mother from the moment I laid eyes on her. If I hadn't heard her voice, I definitely would have thought she was a white woman.

Ray didn't resemble his sisters at all. This always prompted the suspicion about his father whenever he was around his siblings. For the first time, I could definitely understand why this troubled him so much. I, myself didn't see any resemblance between him and his siblings either.

Sure, the red skin tone and fine textured hair was definitely a feature from their mother. Their facial features were nothing alike. Ray's mom had the nerve to question my ethnicity! Shoot, if anyone should have been asking questions, it should have been me after seeing all of them!

I immediately fell in love with his family though. Despite what Ray's mom had done to him with her deception, she still wanted to see him happy. I suppose she was just another woman who had made a mistake. One who didn't quite realize that her one indiscretion caused mental distress in her now adult son.

Upon our arrival, I entered her home to find a picture Ray and I had taken at my girlfriend Zoe's wedding. It was such a beautiful picture of the two of us that not only did she have it on her refrigerator at home, but she told me she proudly displayed it on her desk at work.

Ray and I were a fabulous looking item. We complimented each other very well. Folks would always tell us how attractive a couple we were together. My grandmother, (yes, Grandma Maxine), girlfriends, and even my mommy had this one particular picture of Ray and I displayed proudly.

Ray's mom went out of her way to cook us a mini feast. Oh, we had the spread of a nice "southern meal." I was in heaven. Anyone who knew me at all, knew the way to have my heart required some good "southern home cooking" at some point! You name it and we had it! I loved Ms. Gloria for that meal. If I was coming to that type of a meal on every visit, she definitely qualified as "mother-in-law status."

Ms. Gloria's hospitality was very warm and welcoming. I was happy to be in her home and finally meet the mother who brought life to Ray.

After we got our grub on and took a quick nap, it was time to pick up Ray's only child, Jordyn. He lived with his mom and step-dad a few hours away. I was so sick of being in a vehicle at this point, I was becoming very annoyed.

"What in the hell has gotten into you Summer?" Ray asked.

"I'm car sick Ray," I answered.

It was quite a long drive from Florida to Ray's hometown in Tennessee and then, to have to drive a few more hours. I was done, "stick a fork in me" done!

"Listen, I don't want you to have any moody attitudes around Jordyn, understood?" he asked. I just looked over in his direction without uttering a word.

Jordyn was a very handsome young boy. He had the same beautiful eyes as Ray, but not quite as hazel in color. He was a spitting image of Ray. To my surprise, Jordyn's mother was not at all what I envisioned. She was dark skinned and what most men would call "thick." She wasn't fat, but she definitely wasn't what most would call slender either. It wasn't that she was unattractive. She just wasn't what I had envisioned; bright complexion, petite, prissy little thing with long, straight hair.

Jessica, Jordyn's mother knew Ray very well. Jessica and Ray had been very good friends when Jordyn was conceived. So I was told. Layla and Jessica were still very good friends.

Layla's daughter Kayla and Jordyn were first cousins and Layla felt it was extremely important for them to remain close. Especially, with Ray being away in the military, she felt it was important for Jordyn to have Ray's family as a big part of his life. I had much respect for Layla for being proactive. I also had respect for Jessica as well, for allowing it.

I wasn't invited inside of the home, but Jessica and her husband Joey could feel the tension coming from Ray and me as we waited for them to arrive home. Ray and I had been arguing before their arrival. My unpleasant facial expression said that it had not been a very good day for me at all.

I had previously asked Ray if he had any intentions of introducing me to Jessica and her husband. Ray responded he had no intention to do that. It really upset me because I had made it a point to introduce Ray to Richard, due to Jaden. But, more importantly, I did it out of plain respect.

If he was good enough to meet my son and soon to be ex-husband, why wasn't I good enough to meet his child's mother? I didn't agree with his decision and I made it known. Jordyn did nothing wrong. He appeared to be a sweet and happy kid. I didn't want him to sense any tension between us on the ride back to Ray's mom's house. I tried to make casual conversation with Jordyn by asking him questions. He really didn't seem to show much interest. Soon after, he was fast asleep.

We didn't stay at Ms. Gloria's house that night after watching the boxing fight with Layla and her boyfriend Pete there. Instead, we left Jordyn to play with Kayla and we returned to the motel.

"I'm not going to have you walking around with a chip on your shoulder "Ms. Spoiled Brat," Ray told me. "And why the hell did you feel a need to get my mother involved in our problems!" he yelled.

"Because I don't know what the hell is wrong with you—you crazy delusional man!" I screamed. I simply didn't know how to get through to Ray anymore. Talking to Ray was like talking to a wall. Ray could put up a barrier that a bulldozer couldn't get through! I reached out to Ms. Gloria because I was at a loss concerning why he would agree for me to meet Jessica before our arrival and then, not follow through.

Ms. Gloria was also clueless about why Ray wouldn't introduce us. She knew our relationship was progressing and she didn't see why it was such an issue for Ray either. If Ray and I were just dating, I would not have pressed the issue. But, we weren't just dating. Ray and I had planned a future together at that point.

"When we get back to Florida I'm done Summer," Ray said. He had been as cold as ice when he spoke those words. No expression. No life in him, heartless. A cold mother sucker if you know what I mean. I couldn't believe it! All that man had put me through there was no way I was accepting that "B.S." from him now!! I grabbed the steering wheel as he drove.

"You ready to pull my heart right out of my chest Ray?" I screamed. I was hysterical at that point. "Well, be ready to die Ray," I yelled.

"You have lost your damn mind fool. What has gotten into you woman?" Ray screamed.

"You! You have gotten into my mind, my heart, my soul and my spirit!" I screamed. There was no way Ray was getting off that easily.

I wasn't prepared to die with that fool! I grabbed the wheel just enough to make him think I had lost my mind. I really wasn't crazy at all, but he didn't have to know it! I had always been so timid and had never fought back. Well, I had grown tired of the nonsense he had begun to put me through. It was the same shit I was afraid would happen to me if I had given my heart to him way back when. And look where we were ... the shit was happening just as I was afraid it would.

We had been through hell and high water at that point and he thought he was simply going to walk away! Hell no, was Ray calling it quits! If I had any real common sense and wasn't thinking with my heart, I would have realized it would have been the best decision Ray could have made for me. Often times, we hold on to something old, because we don't trust God that something new will be better! What a grave mistake that can be!

"Mom, Summer has lost her freaking mind," Ray said. Ms. Gloria was sick of us both at that point. We had gone to Tennessee and acted like two straight fools.

"Lord, Lord, Lord," said Ms. Gloria. "What's the problem now Ray?" She asked.

"I can't put up with this foolishness mom," He said. Ms. Gloria remained neutral. Ms. Gloria was no fool. She knew Ray better than anyone. After all, he was her child! She knew his ways oh too well when it came to his relationship history. Instead, she listened to both of us whine and complain.

"I tell you what you both need to do," she said. "Take some cooling off time, away from each other, so you both can think."

Ray had me in a strange little hick, college town and threatened me there ... how in the world did Ms. Gloria seriously expect me to calm down? Ray dropped me off at the motel and he left! I didn't know if he would return or not. All I could do was play the waiting game. About an hour or so later Ray returned. His eyes were bloodshot red. I could tell that he had been crying.

As I arose from the bed, I looked into his face and could see someone who was frightened. Ray was scared I realized. He was terrified.

"Ray honey, talk to me please" I said. Ray just grabbed me and cried uncontrollably in my arms. We both cried. We both had fears. We both had concerns and worries. Neither of us knew what the future promised, but what we did know was that we were in love with each other.

I looked into Ray eyes and I told him "Ray, after Richard I vowed I never wanted to get married in life again! Honey, I love you and I know you have wanted me for the rest of your life from day one and Ray I want the same baby" I told him. Truth was, I couldn't imagine life without Ray being a part of it at that point! We were inseparable! Ray and I held each other that night as though we needed the other to survive.

The next morning it was time to say our goodbyes and head back home.

"I'm really sorry Ms. Gloria for the unnecessary drama. It wasn't quite the first impression I wanted to leave you with" I said apologetically.

"Sweetie I'm a woman, I do understand" she assured me. "And above all, I know my son" she said. She gave me a big hug and told me that I was welcome back anytime. I was relieved that she didn't treat me any different after our ridiculous drama we brought with us.

We picked Jordyn up from Layla's house said our goodbyes there and drove Jordyn back home to his mother. The ride was fun this time. There was lots of laughter and Jordyn was happy he had gotten to see his dad and spend time with his favorite cousin Kayla. We all were "happy little campers."

17

House Warming

$\mathcal{D}$espite the interaction with our families and our many trips, Ray and I still had our arguments. The arguments never seemed to disappear. In fact, they seemed to grow more intense as time went on. One thing I began to realize was, when Ray and I were approaching that second week of not seeing each other, we somehow found things to argue about.

The biggest of our arguments seemed to be about my male friends. I never asked Ray to not have any female friends, but he insisted that I cut all ties with my friends of the opposite sex. Especially, Justin! Justin lived in the same luxury apartment home community as Amber, Gabrielle, and I. I met him one night while Sasha and I were exercising.

"Girl, do you see what I see heading our way?" Sasha asked.

"Girl, do I ever!" I replied.

"Lord, have mercy, Brotha, is fine," we said aloud at the same time.

"Girl, he has the nerve to have bow legs," I said. We shook our heads as though it was a crime to be that fine.

Justin was wearing his headphones. He didn't hear us.

"I'm living in the wrong community," Sasha said. "I need to work out with you more often."

We giggled. Justin was military. The majority of the men in the community were either military personnel or "corporate America" professionals. Justin had dark everything; thick, dark eyebrows, dark eyes, dark hair. His eyes were intoxicating. He had Sasha and I both mesmerized.

However, I had the advantage over Sasha because I was right at his front door. The next morning while we both were off to our daily routines, guess who ran into each other? Yep, you guessed it. It was "night runner" and I. We spotted one another immediately. I was in my SUV and he was walking. I pulled up alongside him as I pushed the window down button to speak. He had the advantage of checking me out this time around. I was wearing a skirt and he was standing up looking into my window, getting a nice view of my long legs.

"Hi, I'm Justin," he said.

"Summer, here," I replied.

"Nice to meet you," we both said. We exchanged casual conversation and phone numbers. Shortly, thereafter, although not immediately … Justin and I arranged to meet for a nice evening to get acquainted. He was by all means a true gentleman. A refreshing, and pleasant feeling overcame me to know that they still existed. He didn't appear to be a player—no childish games. He was a man about his business!

Justin had a music collection like no one else I had met. His music style was unique. He introduced me to the neo soul genre of music. I immediately had respect for him. He was far different from any other man I had ever encountered. Almost, as though he wasn't of this world. I know it sounds crazy, but his thought processes were so deep. I never met anyone who read so many books.

He had furnishings from all over the world from his travels. He didn't speak Ebonics; broken English, he was intelligent. He was a well-traveled, diverse individual. He had two of the most gorgeous daughters.

"Who are these two beauties?" I asked as I held the photo frame in my hands.

"Those are my hearts, my baby girls," Justin said.

"They are absolutely stunning," I said.

Justin brought to my attention very early that he was due to be deployed within two weeks after our initial meeting. We made the most of every minute. We cooked. We listened to majority of his music collection; opening the cd covers and exploring the covers inside and out. We read the lyrics, producers, etc.

I was going to miss Justin, the man I never really had an opportunity to explore close up.

"You promise me that you will write to me, that we'll keep in touch," I demanded.

"No promise necessary Ms. Summer," he said. "I couldn't imagine not getting to know more about the incredible woman before me," he said.

Justin left and he did just as he said. We wrote each other constantly. He was on tour in Japan. There was a lot that Justin hadn't dealt with while home in the states and I was the listening ear who was there to absorb his fears, his aspirations, and his hurts. Although, many miles away in a new and foreign land ... I was his *therapy*. Justin depended on my letters and emails. We had become friends for life.

He made it very clear from the start that we could never be more than friends because he had no confidence in long distance relationships. They didn't and couldn't work for him. Friends, great friends are what we vowed to always remain.

So, how could Ray expect me to just throw my friendship away? Justin was a respectful man. He knew I was involved with Ray. He would never and I do mean *never*, have done anything disrespectful to my relationship in any manner. When I met Justin, Ray was nowhere in the picture–I didn't know a 'Ray' even existed. Innocent email exchanges were all that was left between Justin and I. I was his peace in the midst of his storms. I was his calm water, his place of smooth sailing.

People are placed in our lives … and some, are our "angels unawares." When they come, they enhance and bring positive flowing energy in life's journey. So, why dismiss them as though they were never relevant? Friends are hard to come by. Justin was willing to be a friend from a distance if that meant me being happy with Ray. He wasn't a selfish man. All *he* ever wanted was to know that *I* was *happy*.

I never had one bad word to say when it came to Justin and that's what irritated the hell out of Ray. *Why didn't I have one bad thing to say about this man?* He wondered. *What had we experienced together that was like none other? It was peace he brought—peace Ray.* I thought.

Kirk was the only one Ray was comfortable with accepting. The fact that we were more like brother and sister I'm sure was the determining factor. Kirk was my big brother in my eyes. Kirk wasn't going anywhere. He had always been a shoulder to lean on and a voice of reasoning for me. Ray felt comfortable with Kirk. He saw no threat in him. He actually liked the fact that Kirk seemed protective of me, like a brother was of his sister.

Ray and I determined the time had come for us to begin looking for a place of our own. We needed a place to live outside of the base, a place we could both call home. Ray had come to the realization that there was no outlet or escape from his work on the base as long as he worked *and* lived on base.

Besides, he wanted me to feel comfortable when I would visit. "Slick" Ray also didn't want those hungry, lustful young soldiers and any of the older "perverts" lusting over me! Ray knew exactly what he was doing by moving off base.

Upon my next scheduled visit, our agenda included finding a place to live. We began preparing ourselves for my soon scheduled move to North Carolina.

Months earlier, I set Ray up on a budget and told him the elaborate gifts and trips had to stop. Ray had been throwing away too much money out of the window. None of the gifts he purchased for me were even necessary; he clearly had me wrapped tightly around his pinky by that point in time in our relationship.

I began my search by looking through the "Finder's Guide" for apartments. I was specifically looking for luxury apartment homes. There was no need for us to buy a home because there was no such thing as a permanent location at that stage in Ray's career.

I found a nice, two-bedroom, two-bathroom apartment home in a gated community in one of the most prestigious areas outside of Raleigh. It was beautiful and spacious. The neighborhood was upscale and consisted of business professionals. It was convenient to entertainment, pubs and most importantly, my favorite grocery store.

The apartment had a huge kitchen and plenty of pantry space for bulk food storage. Boy, did Ray believe in saving for rainy days when it came to food! Additionally, the computer desk built into the wall was a very nice addition. It was actually a bonus feature for us because Ray would have a comfortable place to work whenever he had to work from home.

The place had white french doors which led out to the lanai. It also had plenty of closet space for both of our (huge) clothes collections. And, there was more than enough cabinet and drawer cubby for our other necessities. Ray left the decorating and furnishing of the place solely up to me. Boy, did I have fun decorating the place; it actually felt good to step up to the plate and spend my own money furnishing the majority of the apartment. Ray had deserved a financial break for once. The gleam in Ray's eyes and smile on his face when he first saw the decorations and new furnishings said it all, it wasn't just an apartment anymore … it had become our new home!

18

Beach Bums

With Ray and me finally having a place we could both share, I made an effort to take some of the load off of him. Eboni, Kirk and I decided to all drive up together to visit Ray for the Memorial Day holiday weekend. It was quite the road trip!

Eboni was always such a reckless driver. No one ever felt safe with "Wheels of Steel" as we called her, behind the wheel. It was after all, Eboni's 4-Runner truck we drove up in.

"Ok. Y'all ready to hit the road?" Eboni asked.

Kirk and I looked at each other with raised eyebrows and we were both thinking, *Oh Lord, what we have we gotten ourselves into?*

"All I need is my morning coffee and we can ease on down the road," Eboni said. I was already ready for a nap.

"I can't wait to see the new place. Girl, with your taste in interior décor, *I know* it is going to be fabulous!" She said.

I smiled over at her as I shook my head to say, "Thank you for the compliment." Kirk had already fallen asleep in the back seat. Some help he had been!

The miles seemed never ending, as though we would never get there. I told them we didn't have much further to go when I realized we only had about an hour left and that's when Kirk finally lifted his head up to look out the windows.

"Man, this was some drive." Eboni said.

"Yeah, but we are going to have a blast this weekend! You guys ready for Myrtle Beach?" I asked.

I had not been to Myrtle Beach since Sasha and I drove there to pick up her daughter, Briana while Sasha's parents were vacationing there. I loved me some Myrtle Beach! Besides, anything which included a beach was a "thumb's up" in my book!

"Hey, you guys finally made it," Ray said as he welcomed us.

"Yes sweetie," I said as I greeted him with a hug and kiss.

"What up bro-in-law?" Eboni said.

"Hey man, what's good?" Kirk said. Eboni and Kirk went ahead of us and walked around our apartment in awe.

"Summer, when did you have time to do all of this?" Eboni asked. Eboni was cracking up in laughter. "Girl, your behind don't mess around do you?" she said laughing.

"Girl, you already know how I do." I answered.

"Yes, my baby got mad 'skillz'," Ray bragged.

I prepared dinner for us later that evening—after we all had time to relax, of course. Ray had a sports car, an SUV and a motorcycle. I wasn't quite sure how Ray could afford all of his toys; I assumed the military was paying him well, and with him only having Jordyn as a dependent, he didn't have to "cry poor."

Kirk was in absolute heaven when he saw all of Ray's "guy toys." Anything fast or computer games were all right up Kirk's alley! Oh, and how could I forget beautiful women! Ray had quite enough "guy toys" to entertain Kirk the entire visit; I trust too, that Kirk was certainly appreciative.

Dinner was great! All of my friends and family knew I moved around quite nicely in the kitchen. I never had a problem cooking breakfast, lunch or dinner. In fact, whenever I would visit Ray he would always come home to a prepared lunch for his lunch breaks. Dinner was no exception, it was always ready and still hot upon his arrival home in the evenings. He was treated like a king!

"As always, Summer, dinner was great." Eboni said.

"Thank you sweetie." I replied.

"Yeah babe, you put your foot in it." Ray said.

"Thanks Summer." Kirk chimed in.

"You guys are welcome, now, get your lazy behinds up and do the dishes!" I said.

After dinner, Ray took us all out and played "tour guide." Neither Kirk nor Eboni had been to Fort Bragg before. The tour was short lived considering the long drive we had completed earlier that day. Fayetteville, North Carolina was nowhere from Fort Bragg so we went there to a few of the popular entertainment spots—just to stick our heads in for a few minutes.

Beat and exhausted from the long road trip, we were ready to "hit the sack" and call it a wrap!

"Ray, it's time we head home sweetie," I said. Our trip to Myrtle Beach was scheduled that next morning so more driving was in store for us.

"Rise and shine, "privates"!" Ray yelled. His voice was loud and it echoed throughout the entire apartment.

"Baby, it is much too early for all of that noise." I told him.

"Man, why are you yelling so early?" Eboni asked. Eboni was not a morning person at all and I knew her day was not going to start off on the right foot without her morning coffee.

"Baby, please just get some coffee for Eboni and you'll be able to get her to do whatever you need her to do." I said. We all laughed. Kirk had brought his sleeping bag and had slept on the living room floor. He was in his own little world, as usual!

Kirk was ex-military and he definitely had that military mentality. He was an outdoorsman. He reminded me of a black "MacGyver." Kirk had so many gadgets and weird toys that it was unreal. Any time you saw Kirk, you saw some type of hand held game system in his hands. The toys were his "old lady." In short, they were his woman! He was a big kid at heart though, he had a heart of gold. Kirk would help anyone in need if it was within his power.

The morning had come way too quickly for us all. Ready or not, it was time for us to hit the road and head to the beach. The ride was another long one. None of us were ready for the miles ahead. We arrived into Myrtle Beach only to find tons of people and bumper to bumper traffic. People were everywhere!

"The entire United States of America is down here this weekend," Ray said.

"Boy, you so stupid." Eboni told him.

"Oh yeah ... ladies, ladies, ladies in bikinis, we are right on time!" Kirk said. We had such a hard time finding a place to park and with Ray having such a huge SUV, it didn't make finding a parking space any easier. Finally we found a parking spot. We jumped out of the truck and with our feet on the ground, we were ready to hit the strip.

"Eboni, girl did you see those bad shoes over there?" I asked.

"No girl, where?" She asked. Grabbing Ray by the hand, I yanked him towards the shoe shop.

"Do you see those prices Eboni?" I asked. "This can't be the real price, this is definitely a mistake," I said.

"Yep, can you believe it?" she said.

"We must be dreaming!" I told her. "A holiday weekend and clearance prices like this, definitely a deal."

"Yep girl, we are in heaven," Eboni said.

"Excuse me ma'am do you have a *size 7*?" I asked the store attendant.

Kirk and Ray weren't paying us any attention. No, they were way too busy outside of the shop checking out the "hunnies." I glanced out at them every now and then, and each time, just laughed to myself. *Men are such suckers for women.* I thought. I let Ray have his fun with Kirk. Men will be men! I was never one to be the jealous type.

What can you do, you can never stop a grown man or woman from doing whatever they want to do. Right? I was going to get my "look on" too if I had spotted a hunk so I didn't complain one bit! It all was harmless. I knew I had Ray's heart and he had mine. We were there to relax and have some fun and that's what we were doing, period!

Ray stuck his head through the door when he saw me try on a pair of bad, red heels.

"Oh baby, you are definitely getting those. Take those to the register please," he told the attendant.

The beach was way too crowded with people to really enjoy it. And besides, it was hot as heck outside! We were black folks out there so we were *not* trying to get a darn tan!

"Hey you guys, how about we go over to the boardwalk?" I suggested. It was much too hot for us to continue to be out in that heat.

"Where do you want to go Babe?" Ray asked.

"We can head over to the boardwalk," I said.

The Most Loved

19

The Air I Breathe

The boardwalk wasn't far from the beach at all. There were shops, restaurants, putt-putt golf and game activities at the boardwalk. It reminded me of a combination of "Downtown Disney" and "Old Town" in Orlando, Florida.

Ray had previously bought me a nice, digital camera, months earlier. He knew how much I loved capturing special moments. Every time Eboni, Ray or Kirk turned around, the camera was in their face flashing.

"Would you cut it out already Summer?" Ray said.

"Oh sweetie, hush." I said. Ray knew that I was as bad as the paparazzi when it came to picture taking.

As we walked along the boardwalk, I saw everything I wanted and then some! Since putting Ray on a budget, he had become so tight with money; but, the best part of it was that he saw how fast it began to grow. I could hardly get anything out of him anymore. Or shall I say there weren't as many surprises coming my way anymore! It was cool though because we were building a future and that was far more important than anything material. Building a future for our family, our sons, was what mattered most.

Ray and I walked into a watch shop. Watches were Ray's weakness. He had all types of designer watches. As I explored one section of the store, I absolutely fell in love with a really nice GUESS watch. It had diamond chips surrounding a pearl face. It was very narrow in width and was set in a silver, metal band.

"It is simply marvelous honey!" I stated to Ray.

You bet I wanted it. I drooled over it as I slipped into a day dream of having it placed on my wrist. Ray looked over at me with an expression of "don't even think about it" on his face!

Eboni and Kirk came in the watch store as well and were both saying, "Come on guys we are starving, let's eat." Ray 'snapped his fingers in motion' as to say–let's get moving Summer. We walked around for a bit and stumbled across a barbeque joint that was known for some of the best barbeque around.

"You guys ok with eating here?" Eboni asked.

"Yeah, it's cool." we all replied.

We waited for the hostess to come and seat us. Man, did we get our grub on!

"Summer, you are one greedy ass." Ray said.

"Yeah, where does it go?" Eboni asked. They all laughed. I for one didn't think it was too funny being called greedy even if I was damn greedy!

"Man, I'm stuffed," I said.

"You should be, you ate everything except the kitchen sink." Ray said.

We exited the restaurant and began to walk along the boardwalk.

"Girl, look at those fish." Eboni said.

"Oh my goodness—look how big their mouths are," I said. "My Lord, what are they feeding those fish?"

"Yeah, they are everywhere" Eboni said.

"They don't die, they multiply." Ray said. He was such the comedian. He always found something silly to say. I don't even know what those fish were called, all I knew they seemed to fill the entire lake. They were huge and always had their mouths open ready to eat. Just like me!

As we walked along the boardwalk, I suddenly placed my hand over my right temple. I had become faint all of a sudden; something had come over me, right out of nowhere. I began to feel very nauseous. My lungs were slowly closing up and feeling tight inside me.

"Ray honey, we need to leave. I'm feeling really ill." I told him. Eboni rushed to aide me.

"Her ass is always getting damn sick. Can't take her no damn where!" Ray said.

"That's not nice, she can't help it if she is sick." Eboni said.

"Well if she didn't try to eat everything up in the damn restaurant she wouldn't be sick now would she?" He asked.

It hadn't been me being greedy which had made me become ill. No, it was actually my food allergies; the allergies greatly aggravated my asthma.

Most times, I didn't know that I was allergic to certain foods until the reaction would take place.

"Do we need to rush you to the hospital?" Eboni asked. Clearly Eboni was worried to death about me. Well, at least someone was. Ray on the other hand seemed annoyed. We were hours away from Ray's place and I had left my albuterol inhaler back home in Florida. How could I have left my inhaler? Having both allergies and asthma an attack was sure to happen at any point!

"How could you do something so stupid, Summer?" Ray asked.

"Hey man, Ray ease up on her, she's really sick man." Kirk said.

"I don't give a damn. It's her own damn fault." He said.

As we drove along the secluded country back roads of South Carolina heading to North Carolina, I thought, *It will be hours before we get there.* I looked out of the window for comfort. I prayed and asked God to spare my life. *Father, please do not allow this to be my last night alive. Heal me Lord.* I pleaded.

The trees were tall. The roads were dark. The cars were few and far between on the empty road—the road that seemed to lead to nowhere! There was no sign of civilization in those back woods. I coughed, and coughed and gasped for air. I continued to pray and pray. *Lord please spare me.* I pleaded.

Eboni reached over her seat and rubbed my hair. She rubbed my back in an attempt to comfort me. I couldn't say a word—inside I was so grateful for Eboni being there with me.

Light! And finally there was light! Signs of life finally appeared out of nowhere. We began to see lights as we traveled a little further. Finally there was a "Wally World."

"Ray there is a "Wally World," Eboni told him. "Sweetie, do you need medicine?" she asked me.

I muttered, "Yes, I need some strong methanol cough drops with eucalyptus vapor in them." Methanol cough drops and water were great for opening up the breathing passages.

Ray dropped me off right at the front of "Wally World's" door. Eboni jumped out of the truck to escort me indoors. Thank God the ladies restroom was at the front of the store. I ran to the first stall. Everything, and I mean everything that was in me had come out as if from a popped water balloon.

The odor was so overwhelming that Eboni had to leave out of the bathroom. I couldn't stand it myself; a lot of mucus, food and whatever else was coming out! Finally, I was able to find some relief. I found my way to the sink and splashed cold water over my face, head and rinsed my mouth.

I made my way out of the bathroom and there was Eboni outside.

"Are you feeling any better Summer?" she asked.

"Yes, somewhat. I think we can continue heading home now." I told her. We walked over to the truck where Ray and Kirk were.

"You feeling any better Summer?" Kirk asked.

"A little," I mumbled.

"Ok, good." he replied.

Ray didn't say a word. He couldn't even look at me. He didn't want to get so much as close to me. The minute I began to open the truck door to get up into the front seat, I felt my insides coming up again!

"Oh no," I said. I ran to the back of the truck. I began vomiting profusely!

"That girl is so sick! My goodness!" Eboni exclaimed.

All you could see was my head going back and forth in motion. I vomited everything else that was possibly left inside me. Through it all, I could see that Eboni was fuming with anger. She was so furious with Ray.

Finally, there was nothing left inside me to vomit. "I think I'm ok now to head home." I told them.

Empathy was written all over the faces of Kirk and Eboni. Disgust was written all over Ray's face. Knowing Ray the way I did, he was upset because I hadn't come prepared. That military mindset of his reared its ugly head once again.

I already knew his thoughts without him having to say a word to me. I came there unprepared and could have caused my own death! This time, it definitely could have been a life or death situation. A medical emergency could have taken place where I had no help at all, then what? I knew all of that, but the fact remained, I needed him to be by my side regardless of my faults.

With the Lord's help, we finally made it back to his apartment without any more incidents. There had been no more vomiting, no more stops, just a very quiet ride all the way back home.

"Ray, why don't you run Summer a bath?" Eboni suggested. Ray didn't answer.

Instead, he went towards the bathroom. I later walked in behind him. I could see the anger in his eyes. His eyes were red with anger!

I was apologetic to keep the peace between us. I didn't want to argue, I didn't want to fight. All I needed at that moment was tender love and compassion.

"Ray honey, I'm very sorry for tonight." I said.

Reality was, regardless of whether I had caused it on myself or not, he was supposed to be there to care for me. We both owed each other an apology, not just me apologizing to him.

"You know me Summer, and you know why I'm upset." Ray said. "That's all I have to say tonight. Take a bath and get some rest." He told me.

What could I say? There wasn't anything I could say. I took a nice, warm bath and went to bed.

The next morning, Ray was in a much better mood. Eboni had no problem at all expressing to Ray her dislike for the way he treated me the previous night.

The next morning, Eboni immediately let into Ray the minute she saw him.

"I was pissed that Summer would put herself in that situation!" Ray explained.

"I don't care. Summer was sick and you did nothing to try to help her. There was no excuse Ray, none." Eboni snapped.

It was very apparent that Eboni was disappointed and upset with his reaction to my illness. Kirk didn't want to get involved. Instead, Kirk wanted the keys to Ray's sports car. So typical of a man huh? Not to get involved in another man's affair. However, if Kirk had held Ray accountable for his actions then perhaps he would have been embarrassed enough to not want to repeat them. Instead, Kirk chose to opt-out, giving Ray a pass to treat me in a manner that was clearly unsettling to him.

"Hey Ray, what you think about me taking the car for a little cruise? I saw some hunnies along the way that I wouldn't mind checking out...." Kirk said.

Ray knew exactly how it was for a single man. "Are you ok with that?" Ray asked me. It was only fair considering that Kirk was my friend that Ray would ask if I minded.

"If you are cool with it, so am I." I replied to Ray.

"You just be careful Kirk, and be back in a hurry because we need to get on down this road to head back to Florida." I told him.

Well, "Mr. Ladies' Man" didn't come right back! Oh no, he took his sweet little time styling and profiling around the town. Eboni and I paced anxiously, ready to leave and get back home before dark.

"Where is that man?" I asked. I didn't want to concern Ray, but at the same time Kirk had been gone for some time.

Shades on, windows down, and music blaring—who finally decided to pull up? Yep, you got it "Mr. Ladies' Man!" No, he wasn't a "scrub" because he wasn't in the passenger seat of Ray's ride. What he was though, was a man driving an unreturned, borrowed vehicle!

I was not happy at all! Oh he had messed up now, no more joy rides for him!

"Nice of you to finally decide to join us." I said.

"What?" Kirk asked.

"Damn man, did you leave any gas in my car?" Ray asked.

"You good man, don't worry … you good." Kirk replied.

There wasn't much said the entire drive back home. Even though, overall we had a great trip. There was much tension in the truck from me. I was never good at saying goodbye. Even after Ray acted an ass, I wasn't ready to leave him.   He was the air I breathed.

The Most Loved

20

Indecent Exposure

$\mathscr{S}$aint Augustine was our secret "garden of romance." Ray and I arrived and checked into our hotel just before dusk. Whenever and wherever Ray could use his military discount, he would flash his I.D. as though it were a black card!

Ray was intimidated by the fact that he was unable to teach me anything new in the bedroom. He always wondered if he was pleasing me enough in that department. Surely, Ray was satisfying to me in every way, but I wasn't sure what more I could do to convince him of that. It was difficult to fathom why he had so much doubt concerning my satisfaction. My sensual moans and organisms of ecstasy should have been proof enough!

Oh, Ray was quite the pro at grinding his hips. I had no problem "making it rain" to show my gratitude. One night though, too much liquor in Ray's veins entitled others to witness what *only I* had been privileged to view behind closed doors. That particular night was unforgettable–and my girlfriend Nivia was his constant reminder; she vowed to never let him live that one down. He was constantly teased by her… "Ray, you must have been a stripper in your college days."

It was this little hole in the wall club we stumbled into that night, but boy did we all have a blast! All eyes were on Ray on the dance floor when he began to slowly whine his body towards me … even the mens' eyes pierced with curiosity as to which way he would move his body next. The way he made his tight, muscular frame wind was as if he were hypnotizing each of us with every movement!

The women were steaming with heat for him, but the *only* woman Ray saw in the dark of the room was *me*. I loved every single minute of his performance. I could tell by the way Ray's eyes were locked in on my eyes— that the show was intended for *me* that night! He was so sexy with it too. His ability to maneuver like a snake, slowly creeping in on its' prey was a move to be envied by most of the men there.

So, with Ray having such admired skills …"what on God's green earth" were the other women from his past not doing? Why did Ray feel that I was such an educator between the sheets? Was I a "freak?" Sure, I was. It was a Covington family trademark. Most of the folks in my family had high sex drives and were known to be freaky with it! We were a very *sensual* family. In touch with our sensuality is how I preferred to describe it best.

Ray suggested I entertain the idea of us videotaping our lovemaking. I was hesitant initially, it just wasn't my thing … I could see Ray's strong desire to feel like he was bringing something different to our bed so, I eventually agreed.

"Only if you promise to delete it immediately after we are finished," I told him. Trust me, without thinking twice, I made certain the footage was deleted immediately after we finished. As I grabbed the camcorder to go through the footage to ensure everything was in fact deleted, Ray leaped across the room and I mean leaped!

"Dangit man, what's the problem?" I asked. I briefly caught a glimpse of a naked woman pop up on the viewfinder screen as the camcorder was being snatched away from my hands. I knew exactly what the problem had been! Infidelity! Yep, Ray had cheated!

I had no words to speak. All I could do was look crazy.

"Baby, baby, give me that," Ray said.

"I don't think so you asshole," I barked.

"It's not what you think … that happened long before you." He said. Ray came over, calm and collected and laid down beside me on the bed.

"Baby, give me the camcorder you don't want to see that!" He assured me.

"Oh yes hell, I most certainly do!" I yelled.

"Baby, this was before your time," he tried to reassure me.

"Then, why in the hell does it have a November date of this year on it?" I demanded.

"I've been meaning to fix it for some time, it is broken sweetheart," he answered.

"Sweetheart, my ass! Don't play me for a damn fool Ray." I yelled.

"Baby, trust me, that is old," he said.

"Then, why the hell is it on the recorder Ray?" I asked. "You gettin' off on this video?" I asked.

"Girl no, stop trippin'!" he said.

"Oh, you haven't begun to see trippin' yet my dear!" I said.

I pushed his hands away from the recorder and said, "Move Ray, let me see what is on the video."

"No Summer this isn't something you need to see," he promised me.

He was right. That was the last thing I wanted or needed to see! Who would want to see the man who had confessed his love to me freaking another woman?

November? How could this be? I thought. It was during the time Ray had been confessing that I was the *only* woman he wanted and how he wanted to spend the rest of his life with *me*! All of those thoughts ran through my brain like a runaway train.

I made my way to the bathroom shower. I needed for the water to fall on me. I let the water run over and over on my head. With each drop of water, I imagined that it was rain and that the rain was washing away all of the filth between Ray and that naked woman. I tried my best to relieve the pressure from inside me before I "set it off" up in there.

The thoughts wouldn't stop. Everything came back to my memory at that point, and I mean everything! Each time Ray told me he was going to Tennessee to visit his family, and his cell phone reception was bad, was it really now? Hmmm …. or, when he said he had a long day at work and had fallen asleep, and that was the reason he hadn't answered his phone, was it really now Ray? Hmmm …. better yet, when he said he had to do overnight duty on base and had to work all night, did he really now? Hmmm …. that lying "son of a gun" had been lying to me all this time!

I refused to allow Ray to see me cry. He was not going to see my tears or my fears. *No way*! I told myself. I stayed in the bathroom until I was able to regain my composure. I could do it; I just had to convince myself that I could do it. All I needed was to make it through that weekend, that was all! I now had every intention of draining his ass dry that weekend in order to make up for the heartache he had caused me.

I refused to give Ray the satisfaction of a reaction anymore. I thought. When I returned home, I was going to make him wonder if he still had me. I needed to make him wonder and wait in misery for as long as I could hold out. He wanted to play games, "Mr. Love Machine?" *Well, he had picked the right one this time.* I said to myself. Why should I have allowed him to see that I cared, especially when he obviously didn't give a damn about me? But wait, hold up Summer, *Don't men say that they can have sex with someone without caring or loving them?*

Even if that were the case, why was he holding on to that video? I thought. Why hadn't Ray deleted it? He still desired her. There was something more. There had to be something more there. There just had to be!

And he wondered why I had been so protective with my heart. It was bull crap like he was doing that made loving someone, trusting someone; a man at least, almost impossible! Almost, but yet, I loved him. I always gave the man I was with one hundred percent of my trust until he proved me otherwise. And boy, had Ray given me his ass to kiss on that one!

I hadn't been ready to commit, so if what Ray really wanted was to remain single, then, why not just do so? Why did he want me as his wife if he was going to cheat? Was it the distance? I was so confused. I needed answers. I wanted to understand my way through it, past all of the anger and resentment.

I wasn't convinced at all about any of the garbage that came out of Ray's mouth from that point on. I just dropped my head in disgust when he looked at me. A million thoughts raced through my mind. *What if he had been telling me the truth? What if he weren't telling me the truth? Had he been cheating on me all that time?* You know the saying: "The accuser is typically the one who is actually doing the cheating!"

The "video vixen" had nothing on me in terms of her looks, but ironically our bodies were similar. I couldn't really say that I had actually paid any attention to another woman's body before—it wasn't that I was intimated by her at all, hell, my body was flawless. But, what I was intimated by was, the fact that he possibly had been inside of another woman's body while confessing his love for me. *How could he betray me like that? Bastard!*

"Baby, come over here and close your eyes," Ray said.

I walked out of the bathroom wearing nothing, but a towel. "What is it Ray?" I asked. I was so disgusted with that man! I was so very pissed about what my eyes had encountered. I wasn't in the mood at all for any games neither for any more surprises.

"Turn around and open your eyes," he said.

"Ray is this really necessary?" I asked.

"Turn around already, will you?" He asked.

I turned around to find a bright red GUESS box.

"What is this Ray?" I asked. I felt my cheek bones slowly rising. I hated him. He knew me oh too well. It was the same watch I saw and admired when we were in Myrtle Beach.

"Yes babe it's the watch. It has your name written all over it, literally." He said. "Only the best for my baby Summer."

I opened the box. The engraving inside of the watch read: *'With love always.'* If that was what it took for me to get that watch it just wasn't worth the "indecent exposure."

21

Killing Me Softly

The time had grown near, and my scheduled move date wasn't far away at all. Ray started behaving in a very weird manner.

"Sasha, I need you to help me with something," he told her.

"What's that Ray? she asked.

"You know how I can never outsmart that damn friend of yours," he said.

"Yeah, you two are a trip," she said.

"Well, I plan on coming down, but I don't want Summer to know anything about it!" He told her.

"Alright," she said.

A person's pattern of behavior was something I always paid very close attention to. Although, unspoken … if patterns changed, I was very observant to uncover why the change had taken place. Faithfully, Ray and I spoke in the mornings.

"Babe, I have a meeting this morning and I'll probably be in it most of the day," he said that particular day.

There is something about a woman's "intuition" that is a true gift from God. There was an alarm that went off in my head. *Caution! Caution! Caution!* I thought.

Ray was always off from work pretty early in the day. His hours were very consistent. He wasn't one who had to work crazy hours. Sometimes, he would do those "overnights" on the base though. I never tripped, even after the "indecent exposure" episode.

Something within me told me that today, Ray was up to something. I called Ray's phone and received no answer. Within thirty minutes he returned my call.

"Ray what's up babe?" I asked.

"Oh nothing," he said.

"It sounds like you are driving," I said.

"Yeah, I just dropped a soldier off for treatment. I'm heading back to the base now," he said.

It was quitting time from my workday and I was eager to call it a day. That time of day, there was always someone coming down the elevator or walking down the halls getting ready to head out of the back door. I walked down stairs heading to my car. Brandon was also leaving for the day. He was simply a guy who also worked in that particular building.

Brandon and I weren't friends, we just knew of each other from the office. We struck up a conversation engulfing us in laughter as we walked outside to the parking lot. Brandon and I exited the building. I always tried to get a parking spot right in the front row. As we walked towards the parking lot, I looked up and to my surprise there was Ray!

"So now you get personal escorts to your car?" he asked.

Without giving any thought to his smart comment, I quickly ignored it.

"I knew it, I knew it! I knew your behind was up to no good! I had a gut feeling you were heading this way, but I didn't know you were going to show up here at work."

"Obviously, not! Now, who was the guy you were walking with?" he asked.

"Oh that was just Brandon," I replied.

"Brandon, huh" he said.

"Yes, that's just Brandon," I said.

Ray didn't have much to say as he followed me home in his car. On a good day, and normally, Ray would have been calling me harassing me with jokes. *This nonsense really has to stop.* I said to myself. It seemed as though it was getting worse by the week. Ray was growing strong distrust for me. He was always accusing me of this and that with other men.

The minute I turned my head, Ray invaded the privacy of my cell phone by searching for text messages and phone call logs—anything that was possibly from another man. It had become ridiculous at that point. *What more can I do to gain this man's trust?* I thought.

There wasn't a whole lot to do in my hometown. It wasn't the smallest town, but it sure wasn't the largest either. We decided to head to the mall. Ray had a real attitude with me. I hadn't a clue why.

Please don't tell me he is sulking because I walked out of my office building with someone who also worked there. Damn, I can't stop people from leaving the building! I can't not be sociable or friendly to people ... yet, Ray can laugh, play and joke with the entire world! That just wasn't right, it wasn't fair to me. I thought.

As we walked through the mall, I walked a few steps ahead of Ray. I had grown sick of his behavior and I really didn't want to walk along beside him. I saw a group of men walking towards us. All I could think in my mind was, *Oh Lord please don't let them say anything.* As we all approached one another, I made certain that I didn't look in their direction. I heard some mumbles from the men, but I was trying so hard to avoid them that it wasn't even clear to me what had been said.

"Summer, Summer!" Ray called out to me. I turned around to face him. "I can't take your damn ass anywhere!" He said.

"Man, what did I do now?" I asked.

"I know you saw that group of men," he said

"Yeah, and?" I asked.

"You didn't hear their comment?" He asked.

"Apparently not, if I'm asking you," I said. I was so over Ray's behavior and so frustrated!

"They said that, 'I was one blessed man,'" he said.

Can someone tell me please how any man could get upset from another man complimenting him about his woman? I thought. At that point, I was convinced that Ray had completely lost his damn mind.

"You are kidding me, right Ray?" I asked. He just looked at me. That man was so serious. He was "as serious as a heart attack." He didn't crack one smile. I was at such a loss! I had no clue at that point what I could do to make him feel more secure.

"You know Summer, I can't seem to do anything to surprise you," he said.

"How can you say that Ray?" I asked. "You are full of surprises!" I said.

"Your ass always has to know everything! You are too damn smart for your own good ya know!" He said.

Ray was right. I was smart. I was way too smart to be putting myself through such torture. I didn't know what to do. I didn't know how to correct the situation. I wished I could have put things into reverse. We were so far forward at that point!

Ray's visit hadn't been a fun-filled weekend as we had had in the past. Both of our hearts were heavy. I really needed someone to talk to. I needed someone to confide in that evening after Ray headed on the road back home.

"Hey girl, you home?" I asked.

"Yea girl, what's up?" Eboni replied.

"I'm on my way over there." I replied.

"Ok, I'll be here." she said.

"Talk to me, what's on your mind? Spit it out, talk to me girl!" Eboni said.

"What do you think about Ray's and my relationship?" I asked.

She paused for a moment. She looked deep into my eyes with sincerity. I could tell she was thinking hard about her response. She opened her mouth to answer, but stopped herself. She exhaled and said, "I think you would live a life of misery if you stayed together."

There was nothing more Eboni needed to say! She was right, and if anyone could see it, it was Eboni. I hadn't felt any jealousy in her response. Afterall, I considered Eboni my sister. She had nothing but love for me. I knew she always had my best interest at heart. She knew me well enough to know that I came to her for a reason.

"Summer, remember when all of us went to that resort in Orlando?" Eboni asked.

"Yeah, that's when you, your boo, Sasha, her daughter and Ray and I all went to Orlando for the weekend," I replied.

"Do you recall leaving your condo there and coming over to ours in tears?" She asked.

"Yeah, I do" I said.

Eboni in her brilliance had reminded me of the *control*. That Ray's and my relationship was full of *control*! Eboni hated the fact that I wore makeup and wanted me to allow my skin to breathe. I had become self-conscious because of the breakouts I had due to the stress of my divorce. Stress was never a friend of mine. It caused me to breakout and lose weight.

Even through the breakouts Ray didn't feel the need for me to wear any makeup. I went to the makeup counter at the department store in the mall and asked if I could simply buy concealer only. The makeup artist looked at my skin and told me how beautiful my skin was despite the breakouts.

"You have such beautiful skin. Trust me, I see all types of skin and yours is beautiful dear," the attendant said.

"Yes, my boyfriend doesn't feel I need to wear any makeup," I told her.

"That's nonsense, makeup can only enhance your beauty. Sounds like your boyfriend just doesn't want other men checking you out," she told me.

Thinking back ... *wow, even the makeup artist could see signs of control and she knew neither Ray nor I.* I was the only fool that was completely oblivious! Eboni was right. That weekend in Orlando was yet another nightmare!

I went into the bathroom to wash my face before bed to remove the makeup. As I looked through my belongings I noticed that I couldn't find my makeup pouch anywhere.

I opened the bathroom door, "Ray have you seen my makeup?" I asked. He didn't answer me. "Ray!" I yelled.

"What?" he snapped.

"I asked have you seen my makeup pouch?" I said.

"Yeah, I've seen it! I hid that damn makeup from your ass!" He answered.

The moment he confessed to hiding it, war had been declared between the two of us in that condo that night. *That night* it was *me*! I went the hell off on Ray!

"Why would you do something like that?" I asked.

"Because you don't need the shit! I'm tired of you wearing it! Stop hiding behind that damn makeup!" he exclaimed.

I was at a complete loss. I just started crying. I didn't know what to do. He became enraged. He started yelling and screaming at me.

"You got a damn man! It doesn't take all of that Summer, damn!" He said.

"It's not about another man Ray!" I said.

"I don't like the shit!" He said.

When Ray met me I wore makeup. Why was he trying to change me now? I had absolutely no facades! What he saw was what he got! I would have loved to go without makeup. Truth be told, I loved natural beauty and couldn't wait for my face to clear up so that I wouldn't have to wear it. I missed my beautiful clear skin, but the stress from Richard, and now, Ray's ass, had wreaked havoc on my skin!

I thought, *Everything is shown to a person in the beginning. It is up to you to see the person for who they truly are!* I wasn't a "plain Jane." I was a woman who liked to "jazz" it up sometimes.

Compared to my other friends and family I was behind the times when it came to being creative with makeup. I always kept it pretty basic.

Perhaps, if Ray had a conversation with me, instead of him demanding I stopped wearing it, I would have been more receptive to his request. Often times, I found it's "our delivery that kills the gift of possible change." Demanding, ordering, and giving ultimatums gets you nowhere! Humbleness is more appealing and Ray knew nothing about that type of behavior.

22

Countdown ... 9, 8, 7

hirty days and I would officially be a proud resident of Fayetteville, North Carolina. Man, I sure was going to miss Florida's beautiful beaches. Sure, Ray and I could always visit and ultimately after his retirement in six years, we could live there permanently. The days were approaching fast. I was also going to miss my family and close friends.

It was time for a change! The city was no longer large enough for Richard and me. Perhaps, if I left, Richard could finally move on with his life. I avoided him at every turn, but that didn't seem to be enough for peace of mind.

"Are you still communicating with any of your male friends Summer?" Ray asked.

I hesitated and thought before I answered. *Why was he asking me that question?*

"Only by email from time to time," I replied. It had been a night where I needed to clear my head. I parked my car at the beach and just sat in my car with the windows down. There was a nice, cool breeze that night.

"Well, keep f—ing emailing them Summer! I'm done with this shit," he replied angrily.

Before I could get the word "what" out, Ray had hung up the phone. I sat there in silence. I was in total shock and disbelief. This was the same man who I had recently forgave, for cheating on me for his indecent exposure with "Ms. Video Vixen." Yes, upon one of my trips visiting with Ray in North Carolina, I discovered the date on that sex tape was indeed accurate.

God knows I hadn't been looking for anything. I was on Ray's computer one day while he was at work; it was the only computer available. While opened, I looked through his pictures to see what pictures he had saved of us, if any. To my surprise, before my eyes—that same image of the video vixen appeared before me.

I was hurt and I was wounded. The wounds I bore were endless where Ray was concerned. He didn't trust *me* because *he* wasn't trustworthy. He was busted. I had packed my clothes and placed them by the front door. I made the vixen's picture the computer screensaver image. The moment I heard Ray's key enter the lock. I refreshed the screen so that it could be vividly seen once the door opened.

I didn't say a word. He could see by the look in my eyes that I was done! He dropped everything and came over to me crying. Snot ran from his nose as he grabbed me by my legs in an attempt to prevent me from leaving.

"Summer, please don't leave me," he begged.

"I called my family, and they are on their way to pick me up," I told him. My family was less than an hour away. I hadn't called anyone. What I called was Ray's bluff! I certainly didn't want to get my family involved in the drama that we had going on!

"Summer, sweetheart I know I f—ed up," he said. "I have no excuse. It will never happen again. I don't love her. I don't want to marry her. It's you I love," he tried to assure me.

"I can't tell at all Ray!" I screamed. As the saying goes: "Once a cheater always a cheater." I didn't know if that statement was true, or not, but I didn't have the strength to walk away.

"Summer, I truly need you in my life," he said. "I can't do this without you babe."

"Ray this can never happen again or I promise you, I will leave without a trace of you ever hearing from me again," I told him.

It was never ending with Ray. Lie, after lie after lie!

"Layla, I don't know what to do anymore," I said. Ray's sister Layla was someone who I thought would listen. Maybe I could find answers pertaining to why Ray was acting so damn weird.

Ray and I had talked about marriage and kids. Ray already had a son, but I wanted to give him the daughter he never had.

"Listen Summer, Ray is probably just a little nervous about how serious you guys are becoming," she said.

"He has been the main one pushing the envelope Layla," I told her.

"Well, Ray has gone through a lot with his ex-wife," she said.

"His ex what?" I snapped.

"She won't let him see their kids," she said.

"Layla, what in the world are you talking about here? Are we having the same conversation? I'm talking about Ray," I said.

"Yes, and so am I Summer," she said.

The cool breezeway didn't provide enough air for me at that moment. I thought for sure my legs had buckled, and I had begun to faint. An invisible slap popped me right across my face!

"Summer, you there?" she asked.

"I'm speechless," I said.

"I'm sorry sweetie. I didn't have a clue Ray hadn't told you," she responded.

"What happened Layla?" I asked. "I give you my word Ray will never know we had this conversation." I assured her.

"Ray met someone when he was stationed in New York. Their relationship grew very fast, and before anyone knew it, they were married. His wife came from a well-to-do family, and she was extremely spoiled. Ray had his hands full with her and with her mother. Neither of them would allow him to be the man of the household," she explained.

"The three of them left and went overseas to Germany. One day, Ray came home and they all were gone. If that weren't enough she kept him from seeing his son and daughter. He hasn't been able to see his kids for years. After a while Ray just gave up. He really hasn't had a successful relationship since that time," she told me.

"A daughter?" I asked. *Ray had sat there and listened to me time after time talk about giving him the daughter "he never had!"* I thought to myself.

All along, Ray had a daughter after all living in New York. Jordyn really wasn't a "Junior" at all; his son in New York, was in fact "Ray Junior." *How much more can you take Summer? You have gone through hell, high water and back with Ray!* What was left here in this life for me to go through with that man? I was completely numb and broken.

I didn't have to say anything to Ray at all. In fact, Layla did. She called Ray herself to talk with him and tell him that he needed to come clean with me. That's exactly what Ray did. He finally came clean. After he had already been busted, how convenient!

"Summer baby, I know you are thinking here we go again with more sh—t," he said.

Yep, that's exactly what I thought.

"It has been quite an ordeal for me Summer," Ray said. "It had completely messed me up in my head. I didn't think you would accept me with all that baggage," he explained.

Baggage? Was he serious? I was still married. I had not officially received my divorce papers. Although filed, the divorce was not official. And, it was true–I was never living with Richard during the entire separation. There was never one single moment when I gave Richard any hope of us reconciling.

I forgave Ray for all of that, all of it! There was no way I was going to let him just end it like that! I didn't think so! Ray had gotten so far deep into my head! I couldn't see clearly for the life of me. I felt I was losing my mind. I tried to call him over and over again. My calls of course were unanswered. He finally turned the phone completely off.

It was never about me! I wish I had known that then, it was never *you* Summer! Ray had his own demons which operated in his own mind long before he ever set eyes on your beautiful spirit.

The Most Loved

23

It's A Long Road

I was shattered. My bones had been crushed. I couldn't focus. I couldn't concentrate. Every time I would hear the phone ring at work, I jumped in my seat. I was a hot mess! A total emotional wreck! How could Ray do this to me?

Really Summer, you are going to go there huh? Look at everything Ray has done to you already? Hadn't that been enough already girl? My inner spirit was trying to bring some truth to the situation that was surrounding me.

I had lost all sense of reality. I was too far gone. I looked at my phone every minute. Was there a missed call from Ray? I looked at my computer to see if any missed calls had been transferred to my voice mailbox. There was nothing! No missed calls, no voice mails, nothing. I had to walk away from my desk numerous times that morning. I had to fight back tears in order to try to keep my composure at work.

I hadn't been this distraught in my fifteen year relationship with Richard as I had been with Ray! Why was that? I wondered.

I supposed my heart began distancing itself from Richard four years prior to me actually leaving. I had time to brace myself for the closure. My heart had time to gain strength and courage during those last four years.

Ray took me to a place I never thought I would revisit, especially after only two years of being separated from Richard. I never thought I would want to marry another man in life, ever again, after Richard! After all of the negative thoughts Richard tried to put into my spirit, to shatter my self-esteem, I wasn't certain another man could love me the way Richard had.

It wasn't the clothes, jewelry or any of that. It had been the fact that someone loved and cared for me so much that they took care of everything to make certain I had no wants or needs. It was almost like an essential part of your body, a part that you needed to help you function from day to day. That was what my relationship was like with Ray. I had to fix the situation. But, I wasn't quite sure how.

I hadn't eaten anything that previous night nor that morning. I told a co-worker that I felt ill and had to leave for the day. My thirty-day resignation letter had already been received by my manager. I would be resigning due to my engagement and eventual move to North Carolina at that time.

From the moment I got in my car, I knew what I had to do. I put the key in the ignition, and I headed towards the interstate. I had almost a full tank of gas. I just drove. I had traveled the route to Fort Bragg from my hometown several times with Ray; so many times in fact, that I could have traveled it in my sleep.

I was close to South Carolina when I decided to try calling Ray again. He didn't answer.

I left a voice message, "Sweetheart I'm not sure what is going on with you, but I'm heading up there. It's apparent this distance is too much, and I'm just going to prepare to move up there now," I told him.

Shortly thereafter I heard a ring. It was Ray calling. I answered the phone, "Ray?" I asked.

"Summer, don't bring your ass up here!" he said.

"What?" I asked.

"Don't bring your ass up here or I will call the cops!" he told me. "I don't want any trouble."

It had to have been a nightmare! But, I was driving, I was awake! Could this really be happening? I thought. "Or am I losing my mind?" I said aloud.

"Oh, I'm coming Ray! I'm almost in South Carolina," I said.

He didn't say a word. Next thing I heard was a dial tone. He had hung up the phone! I saw the long road ahead....

Everything that followed next took place in slow motion. Suddenly, my body began to drift slowly from the driver's seat, sideways, into the passenger seat. Next, my head followed in sequence with my body. The dashboard was no longer visible. My entire body had slumped over into my passenger bucket seat.

I literally passed out at the wheel of my car. It was nothing short of a miracle from God that my car miraculously guided itself to the right shoulder of the highway. Semi tractor-trailers zoomed by me as they brushed air underneath my sports car, slowly shaking it.

Each time I entered my vehicle, I made it a habit to pray that God would "encamp his angels all around my path to protect me from dangers seen and unseen." It was apparent God had done just that and so much more!

I hadn't eaten anything, I hadn't drank anything and the stress alone could have sent me into an asthma attack at any moment. I wasn't sure how long I had been passed out when I woke up. I didn't know where I was. It took me a moment to regroup and gather myself. At that precise moment, I knew I didn't have any choice except to call my family for help!

Even though I survived passing out at the wheel, surely, I had a death sentence coming my way by my family for doing something so stupid! I knew they were going to kill me for sure!

"Where are you Summer?" Traci asked. I called my cousin Traci up in Raleigh to let her know what had occurred.

"Are you driving Summer?" she asked.

"Yes, I just started driving again," I answered.

"Ok, you don't need to do that!" she said.

My determination prevented the tears from falling previously, but, they finally found an escape and they wouldn't stop!

"I can't believe this is happening Traci! How could anyone do this to someone?" I asked.

"I don't know sweetie," she said. "Don't worry about that right now. We need to get you safe."

"I'm going to call my mom and your mom," she said.

"Traci please don't call my mom," I begged.

"Summer, you aren't having auntie kill me girl!" she said. "She needs to know where you are. Summer I need you to find the nearest hospital sweetie."

I didn't think about a hospital. I thought about getting to Ray to find out what was going on with that man. I had made it that far and I wasn't turning back!

God knew if it meant costing me my life that I needed answers. And I needed them yesterday! I wasn't going to go and sit in some lonely, cold and strange emergency room. No, I was going to be in the comfort of Ray's and my own home.

24

Open Up

$\mathcal{I}$t was only by the grace of God that I finally made it to Ray's place safely. I followed someone into the main entrance gate of the complex where Ray resided. I pulled up outside of his building to find Ray's two vehicles and his motorcycle parked there.

"That lying snake was home," I said. He wasn't out of town as he had previously claimed earlier that day in attempt to discourage me from coming. Ray was home!

I knocked on the front door. He didn't answer.

"I know you are in there Ray!" I said. "Let me in!"

"What are you doing here Summer?" he shouted through the door.

"You know damn well why I'm here Ray now open this door!" I said.

"Go home Summer!" he said.

"I'm not going to talk to you through this door—now open up Ray!" I said. I started banging on the front door. "Open this door!" I yelled.

"If you don't leave Summer I will have to call the police," he said. "I can't have you around here with all of that noise!"

"Go ahead call them, by the time they get here we both will need them," I replied.

Thoughts of smashing his windows, keying his car, and throwing a brick through his french doors ran through my mind. In fact, every thought imaginable went racing through my mind. That just wasn't me though; it wasn't me, Summer.

I had some major issues going on inside of me, but no man was worth me going to jail, I knew that much! I was many, many things, but I wasn't completely insane at that moment. Or was I? I couldn't do that to my family! That piece of dirt wasn't worth me ruining my clean record–that I knew for sure.

I walked around to the lanai and tried looking through the french doors and windows in the back. I could hear the upstairs neighbors on their patio. There were two women enjoying the nice, evening breeze.

People were out exercising, walking their dogs and playing with their toddlers. Being outside was once something Ray and I also enjoyed together. I could remember Ray laying back in the lounger outside smoking a cigar, as I would walk around the manmade lake for exercise.

I was tired, exhausted and was barely able to breathe at that point. I finally saw Ray's head peek out of his bedroom window. I didn't see any other shadows as I suspected. I thought for sure that I would. There was no one else in there except Ray! In my heart I was hoping that Ray had possibly found someone else and moved them in there. That would have been a more bearable explanation for his bizarre behavior towards me.

Ray had sat there in bed while I was locked out on the outside. He held his computer in his lap. He refused to look at me! I tapped on the window. I saw no evidence of any one having been there. Everything in there was exactly the way I had left it. My clothes, my furnishing, my belongings were there in clear sight.

"Ray, I can't breathe—my asthma," I said. It began getting cool outside and I wasn't prepared to be outdoors at that hour.

"Ray, can you please check to see if one of my inhalers is inside there or in one of the vehicles?" I begged. After everything that had happened, I *hadn't* learned to ensure my inhaler was with me at all times. He didn't get up immediately. Ray waited until he couldn't hear me anymore. I heard the front door open. I was in the back lying in one of the patio lounge chairs on the lanai. I was too weak to even get up to confront him. I was sinking and sinking fast!

"I don't see any!" he said.

"Can you please just let me inside until my aunt gets here?" I begged. "I won't say anything to you!" I was completely exhausted. I had no energy left to fight with Ray. I just really needed a warm place at that moment. I needed to get indoors.

"I'll go in the guest bedroom" I told him. "We don't even have to look at each other." I promised. The right thing to do would have been for him to leave, and allow me to stay there until my aunt arrived.

My mommy and Ray were close. She really liked him a lot. Of course, she had no idea the extent of all that was going on in our relationship. I was a very private person. As I sat outside, I could hear my mommy's voice on Ray's answering machine; he ignored it, ring after ring.

"Ray, could you please call me so we can talk?" she asked.

I sat outside thinking, *I can't put my family through this!* Why couldn't I walk away? I just couldn't fathom, for the life of me, why I was putting up with his craziness. Sure, I was in love, no doubt, and of course, love will make you do some crazy things. I realized that

Ray had damaged my self-esteem. I allowed him to take me to a very, very low place. *How could I?*

The upstairs neighbor yelled down to me, "Are you ok?" she asked.

"No, I am not!" I said.

She didn't know me from Eve. I walked out onto the grassy area so that I could see who was speaking to me from above.

"Will he not allow you in?" she asked.

"No, he will not!" I answered.

She waved for me to come upstairs. I looked a complete mess! My contacts were barely in; they were cloudy from all of the crying, and my mascara was smeared all over my face and around my eyes. My hair was standing up on the top of my head.

"Do you have family here?" she asked.

"No, I drove here from Florida" I said.

"You drove all the way from Florida and he won't allow you in?" she asked. Her husband was there.

"Yes, I don't know what to think" I said. "My aunt is on her way here from Raleigh" I told the couple.

The community was predominately white with very few blacks residing in it. A quick glance around the apartment and I could see the signs of order and discipline. Her husband was definitely military as well.

"Thank you so much for offering to help me" I told them.

"I heard you pleading with him to allow you in" she said. "When you said you had asthma it frightened me, I just can't believe he wouldn't open the door!" she exclaimed. She wasn't trying to be hurtful by reiterating his total lack of concern; she was simply blown away by his behavior.

"Is there anything we can get for you?" she asked.

"Yes, please tell me you have some contact lens solution" I said. I couldn't see a lick without my contacts or glasses.

"I'm sure my husband has something," she said. I was able to cleanse my contacts and wash my face up a bit with warm water. I was very thankful for their help. Angels. Angels. Angels. God was definitely watching out for me, and had sent his angels to watch over me that day!

"My aunt is en route so I better head over to my car to look out for her" I said.

"You sure?" she asked. "I'm Sue and that's my husband Rick by the way," she said.

"And I'm Summer," I said. "It was a pleasure meeting both of you and I am so very sorry for getting you involved."

"I'm sorry you had to go through this Summer," Sue said. "Take care of yourself."

"I will and have a great night guys," I said. "God bless."

The Most Loved

25

Bone Deep

*J*ust as bone needs marrow, that's how badly I needed Ray. He was my Vitamin D. I needed him to help me grow! It took two, long hard weeks of me burying myself under the covers, not eating and slowly wasting away for my mommy to finally get my attention!

My mommy's concern for me grew with each day.

"Summer, you aren't eating anything" she said. "I know it hurts badly, and as a mother, it hurts me so bad to see you in so much pain and not be able to do anything." I knew it was hurting my mommy to see me in such despair. *That bastard. How could he do this do us?* I thought.

My mommy had always been there for me. With me also being a mother, I couldn't bear the thought of seeing Jaden go through anyone hurting him in such a manner. I avoided any friends or family for weeks. The thought of Jaden seeing me in that state definitely wasn't an option. No way!

"Summer, I think you need to give your counselor a call," she said. "You really are frightening me, and I don't want to lose you."

I could truly see the pain in my mommy's eyes! I couldn't put my loved ones through this a minute longer, especially my mommy. I had to get help! My counselor Debra agreed to see me three times a week for the first couple of weeks. She knew I had been through so much with Richard and that I was really fragile at that point!

Thought after thought raced through my head. *Despite all of the mental anguish, Ray and I had been friends. Ray I thought, listened. I thought he understood me. I thought Ray truly knew who I was as a person. I believed that Ray would always take care of me.*

"Summer, Ray is gone," Debra said. "Time to let Ray go! This is about Summer! You didn't fall in love with Ray overnight. It will take time. Losing someone in a relationship is no different than losing someone through death. You must mourn, you must go through the grieving process Summer. You will get better, you are strong! Summer, you have the strength of God residing in you. It won't be by your strength alone that you will make it through this, but lean on God. Cast it upon God, Summer!"

Debra saw many patients who had far more serious issues than I had. She knew I had been through far worse with Richard and was still standing, without even an ounce of medication being prescribed to me. I just needed a voice of reason. Someone who was distanced from the situation. Debra was the answer.

It was time to say goodbye to Ray. People thought I lived the life that some can only dream about, but they weren't there. They didn't see. They didn't hear. They didn't feel; didn't feel the pain, the struggle, the tears, the years! They didn't know my story, they only saw what they thought was the glory.

I had to get back to a good place. A place where I was content, and happy again. I was determined to have my smile back and get back to living and enjoying life again. I could no longer think about what used to be, but it had become time to create new memories. A new season in my life, if you will. I had those "Amazing Graces" in my life; Eboni, Zoe, Madison, Amber, Gabrielle and Sasha; they were all still there for me. I could always count on them to bring a smile to my face and lift my spirits. They helped bounce me back from my heartbreak, the blows to my shattered bones. Although, it would take *years* later for my heart to fully recover from the damage of Ray, I never gave up on love. *I will always be a true romantic at heart.* I thought.

The Most Loved

26

Mirror, Mirror

*S*earching my soul hadn't been easy, but it was necessary after *many* years of disappointment and heartache. There were questions that I felt I needed answered by God. Thinking, "*I never want to love this way again*" after Richard to "*love overboard" with Ray*— and now, *"where do we go from here"* with Santos. *I must find an escape, any reason to leave here! It never could work between us. I wasn't ready for what God had in store for me,* I thought.

"Santos, it's freezing in here!" I yelled. My voice echoed through the cold, empty halls. Being the perfect gentleman that he was, Santos allowed me to sleep in his bed. The previous night he graciously took his appropriate place in his favorite spot, the den.

He mumbled, "Okay." His head looking like a ball in a catcher's mitt, fell safely back inside the soft cushions of the couch.

Cold temperatures were never a friend of mine. *It's cold in here*, I convinced myself. *Stop it Summer, just stop it.* I thought. I tried to find any old excuse why I had to leave him. Any reason at all, to get out of there immediately! I moved frantically around the room, like a fire alarm had been set off! I grabbed my belongings as I took a quick peek around the corner. Slowly, I peeped my head out to see if Santos was counting sheep.

"Yesss, out like a light!" I whispered.

I tiptoed out unto the cold tile floors, trying my best to be as quiet as a country farm mouse. Finally, I made it to the front door. My sweaty palm wrapped the door knob tightly. I was careful not to make one solitary sound as I ran out the front door. I sprinted, as if I were in a twenty yard dash. I ran for dear life, straight to my car!

"Man," I shouted quietly. He had me fenced inside the driveway.

I reached for the gate handle, "Yes! It's unlocked!" I muttered excitedly as I lifted the latch.

I was careful to open the gate slowly. I exhaled a huge sigh of relief. As my butt hit the bucket seats in my sports car, I quietly backed the car out of the driveway.

What am I doing? I asked myself. "Honk, honk" a driver behind me honked for me to get moving. I finally began to accelerate forward.

As I drove, I thought back to the very first encounter between Santos and I. He represented "the finer things in life"; he drove a European luxury car, he was a homeowner, distinguished and always elegantly dressed– that was Santos. Alluring and intriguing; he was a unique man to me, in every way!

Staring at Santos was my very own reflection in the mirror—we were alike in so many ways. Sure, Santos was warm-spirited and kind, but I could tell, just like me, when he invested in you, he expected you to give your all. Anything short of that, would have been a cent too short for him. If Santos had any inkling at any point that you were holding out emotionally, he would be out like a jack rabbit without hesitation!

Santos had done absolutely no wrong at all. No, the blame was all laid out on Summer's lap this time. Yep, this one was all yours Ms. Summer. Way to go! Yeah, well at least I was woman enough to admit it. I took full responsibility for this total mishap. *Total mishap? It wasn't no damn mishap Summer!* I thought to myself. It was my own stupid fear of someone actually being able to love me.

Poor Santos, what had he done to deserve that from me? Was he attractive? Yes ma'am! *They* were always very attractive, check mark. Nice body, check mark. The most adorable smile with dimples, no kids, no baggage; check, check, check!

Santos was a great composer of music. His beats were fierce! It was his passion.

"Man, I blew it." I slapped my hand against my forehead and cried with heartache.

Damn, Damn, Damn! The damage was done! Santos was long gone. How could I have blown this one? Santos was heaven sent. Everything I prayed and asked God for, He sent down to me in perfect order. Everything, just the way I liked it and, to top it off, delivered right on time!

Apparently, not in Summer's time though. That was way too eerie, sort of creepy if you had asked me. I was completely nuts to mess this one up. I hadn't healed at all; my scars still ran very deep. And, I had no idea, just how deep....

"Earth to Summer," Santos said.

"I'm so sorry, I just find this incredibly hard to believe." I told him. "Your last name is what again?" I asked nervously. "When is your date of birth?" I asked, alarmed. I further asked for more details. "Do you mind if I see some identification please?" I reached to grab something, anything! *Could this really have been happening? Was it possible that I actually have a twin who was from Europe?* I thought.

Santos, being a former model was handsome; he was fine, intelligent, and witty. Hell, he was just like me! I tried desperately to piece the puzzle all together.   Well, let's see … my father was in the military.   Did my parents secretly put him up for adoption or did someone steal him at birth? *Was any of that logical?* I wondered.

"Are you nuts?" I asked myself aloud.

"Excuse me?" Santos asked. "Summer, get a grip, I mean it really isn't that serious," he said. Correcting himself he said, "Ok, excuse me—this really is bizarre, the many similarities in our lives, but what can we do at this point? Summer, I am really feeling you babe." Santos tried his best to encourage me to give us a chance to get to know one another.

I recall telling him, "Here's the deal Santos ... you see I had this little talk with God giving him my list of desires in a mate. This list was compiled of only three things: 1. Me, not having to change my last name, 2. Sending me a man who would fully compliment me, and 3. A man who would love me as Christ loves the church," I explained.

"Whoa, now that is reeeal deep Summer, not only do we have the same last name, but also the exact date of birth," he said.

"I am lost for words." Santos said dumbfounded.

"Yeah, you think God hears my prayers?" I asked.

We laughed. "I have a proposal," he said.

"Damn, already?" I said as I laughed jokingly.

"Let's forget if only for a moment, how or why we met," he said. "Can you just allow us to simply enjoy the beautiful presence of one another's company and this meal?" he asked. He smiled at me with those deep chiseled dimples.

"It's a deal handsome, let's grub." I said as I smiled back at him.

———

Ring, ring, ring ... I looked down at my phone, afraid to answer. *Answer the phone. Summer answer the phone.* I convinced myself.

"Where are you? Summer, where are you?" Santos said on the other end of the phone. Clearly Santos was upset.

"I had to leave," I answered nervously.

"You had to leave?" He asked confused. "Summer, we had the entire day planned," he said. "What are you doing Summer?" I could tell he must have been in total disbelief, trying to understand.

"I will come back later." I said, trying to reassure him.

"Summer, you just got up and left without a word ... why would you do that? Why didn't you wake me up?"

he asked. "I have never seen or experienced anything like this before!" His tone was serious so I knew he was livid.

Quietness filled the air of my car; almost as if it were thick, dark, black smoke smothering me. I felt like I was dying a slow death, gasping for air, for life. I proceeded to drive 80 miles per hour down the highway in my sports car. I accelerated my speed as I watched the miles escape me.

"I have to get far away." I repeated to myself. Eventually, the phone went dead. All I heard was a faint, beep, beep, beep ....

Who? What? When? Where? Why? How? Those were questions I'm sure Santos wanted answers to. Who? That was, *Garrett*. What? That was, *"This is too good to be true!"* When? That was, *prior to* meeting Santos. Where? That was, *deep within the cries of my abandoned womb*. Why? *Everything happens for a reason*, that's why! And finally, How? *He*, Garrett, came like a thief in the night, stealing my heart away … he ripped it right out of my chest wall ... *Never again could something too real to be true, actually be real*. I thought. All thanks to Garrett.

Pen firmly in my hand–my journal entry read … *Time and time again you run away like a thief in the night— running in fear for dear life… the past is gone, the present is here—when are you going to allow a new love to embrace you, come near. Every man isn't Garrett.*

Yes, God knows how much you loved him, but God wants to heal you Summer. Garrett is never coming back for you! Stop holding on to a pipe dream—it's hollow girl, those words of Garrett's are empty, unfulfilled promises. He will never make good on any of them. I know you want to believe that you could not have been wrong, but it's "time to face the music." Summer, you were dead wrong ... you were wrong about Garrett, period! Was I wrong? Where and when did our love go wrong, Garrett?! I want to know....

27

New York, New York

he "friendly skies" had become my friend. During my travels, I was always meeting new people; at the airport, on the plane, in the cities.

With my fun, bubbly and upbeat personality, it was hard not to engage in conversation with someone. It was so exciting experiencing a diversity of cultures, and gaining a wealth of information from various sources throughout my travels.

I was a firm believer that "every day of our lives we should learn something new that we didn't know the prior day." For me, that also included meeting someone new. Business cards, email addresses and phone number exchanges were prevalent with both women and men during my travels. And meeting Garrett was no different … than meeting anyone else for that matter. Well, at least not initially.

"I'm sorry Summer, but you deserve better than me." If Summer had heard it once, you best believe I had definitely heard it twice. "Boogie down "Bronx!" Yeah, those guys had much "flava." I didn't always think that way of New Yorkers. In fact, it was just the opposite. Oh no, my opinion had always been that New Yorkers were a rude and extremely obnoxious group of people.

I was really afraid of New York men especially! They were angry, controlling and verbally abusive men; if anyone asked me, that's what I truly believed. Men, who in my mindset, were mad at the world for no apparent reason. That was the picture I had painted in my head ... that a New Yorker could have absolutely no love for Summer, and Summer definitely had absolutely no love at all in return.

For the very first time in my life, I was intimidated by a man. A man who said he was from New York, that was! Then, I met a New York man who demonstrated sensitivity. It was then, and only then, that my opinion changed.

Once I met Garrett, there was no distance known to man that could ever keep us apart. If Garrett and I never spoke or saw one another in life again, we both knew that what we shared would forever live in each other's heart....

28

Who Is He?

How could I ever forget that man after all of this? Our relationship was a bond not easily broken through a "seed of life" that never would come to fruition.

Perry Ellis, Stacy Adams, Italian cut slacks and suits, Robert Weil, Movado and Michael Kors watches … he wore colors that perfectly matched his smooth, brown skin tone; tan, brown, blue, black and peach were all colors that complimented his complexion nicely.

He wore Size 12 shoes; Kenneth Cole, Aldo, and Clarks. His shirts, 18 1/2 with a 34/35 sleeve, simply, XXL. Garrett's waist was 40 inches, and his pant length was 32. Although, his waist wasn't actually a 40, a 40 waist was necessary in his case, in order to get the pants over his muscular thighs! Garrett's swagger was simply intoxicating.

I remember him saying, "Now if I tell ya my all time, favorite song, as far as deepness, I would definitely have to wife ya! That song, along with a candle lit room, dinner, a Jacuzzi awaiting us, conversation, feeding you chocolate covered strawberries along with smooth wine … that would have the two of us falling asleep together. But, by the time we awoke, we'd have a family." He assured me. "Ya feel me Summer?" He asked with his thick New York accent.

"That's what I call dangerous material and use only with the most extreme caution." He continued. "Now if you hear me play that song ya might wanna run for the hills because I'm not responsible for what happens after that. Just know, I tend to black out into this mad loving individual and the next thing I know ... we'll hold that thought for now." Garrett said to me as he chuckled in laughter.   Well, not only did Garrett share the name of that song, but he also shared the lyrics.

What is the famous saying that I was all too familiar with? "Fools rush in." Every night, regardless of what was going on in Garrett's life, he made time for me. Faithfully, we read scripture together at night and prayed before bedtime. I was certain Garrett shared a part of himself with me that he perhaps had not shared with anyone else.

Garrett had this longing to understand his purpose in life. Years of military experience and being raised in "da Bronx", he was definitely not one to toy with. He was a man who had passion and love for his family and one who was always there for his friends. I was able to see all of that in Garrett.

Garrett had no biological children of his own. He did choose to raise his ex-wife's son as if he were his own though. He had been very clear about his love for this young man from the start and made it clear that he wanted to have an important role in his life. I placed so much value in knowing Garrett's opinion. *Why? Why? Why did I value Garrett so? Was it because I was in love?*

Shoot, this wasn't the first time I had been in love, madly in love for that matter! This time was different though, Garrett was different. Did astrology play a part? Was it something in the stars? *The universe perhaps?* I wondered. Garrett and I both were Scorpios, did this have something to do with it or was there something more?

There was only one other person in this world who knew how much Garrett meant to me other than God of course; and that one person was my home girl Sasha. Sasha had never been easy on the men in my life that she had met. Perhaps, it had to do with the pact we made; that we would always look out for one another, when it came to men especially!

We all have been hurt, show me a woman who hadn't and I'll show you one who is a liar. Sasha made it no secret that Ray would always remain her favorite. Of course, Sasha had no clue of all the torment he put me through, despite how close we all were–I did not tell them everything. Most often, they only saw the gifts and the love Ray expressed.

However, after meeting Garrett for the first time, she quickly gave me her approval. He was "brother-in-law material" and "a keeper." That was Sasha's first impression of Garrett, she assured me.

Upon Sasha and Garrett's first time meeting, they went at it hard! One would have thought they had known each other for years. I looked at them both with raised eyebrows. Must be a northern thing, going hard that was! Being born and raised in the south, we were a little more reserved initially. Very friendly, with warm hospitality, but southerners were definitely more discreet with insults for sure!

Sasha being a typical Gemini, she definitely had a split personality and Garrett picked up on it instantly. That was my boo, sharp as a whistle, he could detect anything. I was shocked because Sasha was very hard to read at times. One never truly knew what was going through her mind. Especially where men were concerned, no doubt!

29

Pampering Anyone?

"I woke up in the middle of the night to find a very pleasant surprise on my phone ... and all I can say, was that the rest of that night was a very peaceful sleep, which included a smile on my face." Garrett said to me.

"I looked at the pictures again once I woke up. I imagined that you were actually in the room with me as I got dressed for work and the world seemed alright!" He said.

It felt like a dream to me; being with a man who was so strong and so tough and, could allow little ole' me to melt him down in such a way.

Garrett had no problem pouring his heart out to me. "I got in my car and all I could think about was you, and how I really enjoyed the conversation," he said.

"I know it's funny, but looking at it, those are the things that bring you close. See, I'd add a little sexiness to it but, that would be between me and you," he said.

Garrett and I talked every day on the phone. He would get just as mushy as I would.

"If that kind of information were to get out, then, my image would be shot," he said. Oh no, he never wanted his peeps to know what an affect I had on his emotions. It was all good. I knew his heart was sincere.

"Honestly, though I'd pamper the hell out of you." Garrett said. "Hugs, kisses and coming up behind you out of nowhere and whisper whatever sweet word that came to mind in your ear," he said. I took in every ounce of what Garrett was pouring into my spirit.

"Everyone, but mostly you, would see how you are truly loved." He'd tell me. Garrett's profession of his love to me was welcomed. It was truly appreciated. "I was just playing with this idea this morning and wrote it down, but it needs some touching up," he said. "I have the concept, but will play with it some more to refine it. The title of it is 'My Offer':

A man of wealth can shower you with a lifetime of monetary value; I offer you a day to carry your burden of life's labor.

A wealthy man can purchase you a lifetime's amount of luxury transportation; I offer you a long walk and laughter as we dream of our travel.

A wealthy man can wine and dine you in the finest of restaurants; I offer you a candlelit dinner on a blanket.

A wealthy man can take you on expensive vacations around the world; I offer a piggy-back ride around the block while we laugh together.

A wealthy man can purchase you a 15 carat engagement ring and a million dollar wedding;

I offer you my heart and a lifetime promise and steadfast commitment.

"Wow, babe that was absolutely beautiful!" I said. "You have me down here in tears. Now, I can't be the only one over here with my heart melting away Mr. Poet. You know how I love to dabble with the pen myself. Here goes," I read to him:

I didn't get a wink of sleep last night … Tossed and turned until broad daylight … Visions of "him" invading my brain … Cascading through my entity as deep as the ocean's waves… My head, throbbing in dismay… Why can't my mind stop this madness, kneel down and simply pray? Night after night, day after day ... The longing for "him" will not fade away ... The moment my head lay down to rest "he" is implanted, clinging onto my dreams....

Dreams of my life before me in a cloud; relationship after relationship and yet, he remains unfound ... This man with no face could have been there on any given day

... My God, so nervous if I were to see "him" what would I even say? Would I tell him ... that he invades my dreams as a shadow throughout my nights? As I long for him I grab my pillow and hold it snug and tight; struggling to get some sleep, please Lord just this one night! Should I tell him, that although I had never seen his face today he is the very vision for which I have always prayed? Would I tell him, that at a distance I have watched in admiration, the man that God so graciously made? Should I tell him, that my heartaches were preparing me how to love "him" unconditionally? Would I tell him, that I know he is not perfect, but he is the perfect one to help rebuild me emotionally? Should I tell him, this day I hoped would happen that it'd be "us" together happily? Would I tell him, it is "he" who has made my heart beats skip a little faster?

Should I tell him, it is "he" who has filled my life with so much joy and laughter? Should I tell him, that when God made me, I was complete when he made you? My long awaited dream, my love, my destiny!!!

30

Someone Call 911

A contractor for the federal government was how Garrett made his living in D.C. Intriguing and adventurous I found Garrett's life to be. His job was such a mystery to everyone and it was extremely fascinating to me. The mystery of it all that was!

I recall one of Garrett's childhood friends Vince, also from New York saying, "Garrett would get a phone call from his job while visiting us, and off he would disappear. No one knew the direction that he went," Vince said.

There wasn't much at all that Garrett could share with me about his job at that time. At that moment, it was okay that he didn't. I accepted that. I trusted Garrett without any doubts. I never felt insecure, suspicious or unloved. Well, initially I didn't.

Garrett was a man of authority. He had military, law enforcement and now, secret service experience. He wore many hats. Surely, Garrett was a man whose gift was to protect and serve others; and, there was nothing sexier to me than a man in uniform. Garrett protected others, but who was going to protect him from the intoxication of my love?

I was my father's daughter. My father could get any woman he wanted. And I could get any man I wanted. Order and discipline were what I found most attractive in men of the authority. Garrett was all of that to me and then some. "Handsome and charming" a grown ass man described him perfectly.

Garrett was over six feet tall and over 200 pounds of pure muscle. Garrett's stature was the same as most NFL players—strong and durable! "Luv" was Garrett's term of endearment for me; that's what he called me via phone, text, email or in person.

Garrett lived close to my girlfriend, Sasha in D.C. I could always kill two birds with one stone while visiting Washington. Traveling there had become quite the norm for me.

"Garrett, where are you? My flight landed almost an hour ago," I snapped at him.

"Luv, I'm almost there I'm stuck in this traffic jam," he said.

I didn't give a flying kite. I was ready to relax and unwind. "Will this man hurry up!" I said. The entire day had been an extremely exhausting day, and I had an exceptionally long flight!

I could immediately tell that I had pissed Garrett off by the way he pulled up along the curbside with his black, big bodied Benz. Garrett exited the vehicle and barely looked in my direction. He gathered my luggage and mumbled something towards me. I got in the car without saying a word. I had no idea where we were going and I knew very little about D.C.

If it weren't for the music playing through the sound system, no one would have known that he had a passenger. Complete silence filled the interior of the car. There was no exchange, no conversation. Garrett and I were both Scorpios. Characteristically it's quite a shame that we weren't born twins, we were so much alike. At that moment, we both were behaving stubbornly, like two spoiled brats!

A very beautiful fall night, I marveled at it as we cruised the highways of D.C. And there we were, behaving like our shoe sizes. I looked out of the window and thought ... *I could have celebrated my birthday in Florida instead of dealing with this nonsense!*

"May I ask where we are going?" I finally uttered to Garrett. Fear of him driving me straight to Sasha's house and dropping my lil' ass off at her doorstep, I felt I had to make a sad attempt at conversation.

"It's not much farther, I am taking you to a nearby town." He said.

Oh Lord, my mind began to race. Fear poured over me. I thought, *He probably was going to ditch me in some nearby town. Fool, get a clue, that man wouldn't do that to you.* I convinced myself. *Nah, Garrett wouldn't do that.* It was my birthday, and knowing Garrett, he probably had something planned.

31

Surprise, Surprise

arrett was always full of surprises! But, were my eyes deceiving me this time? Is this place for real? My eyes blinked. I blinked again to make sure I wasn't dreaming. "Oh my gosh, this is heavenly." I said. My eyes began to fill with tears. It was my night, my night to be treated like Cinderella. No, it wasn't a dream. It was real. Garrett was real. He was real special.

Soft, dimly lit lights pierced through the trees which hovered over the sidewalks. It was as if we had been taken back to another place in time; a time when courtship existed between a man and a woman, a time when people weren't having relations on the first date, a time when a man wasn't afraid to show his love for a woman.

A time when a man was proud to show respect towards his woman; he wore it like a badge of honor. We had escaped to a time when love was innocent, gentle and pure. It indeed, was a time that I would always remember and never, ever forget!

The town was small and secluded; secluded from the political noise that rang out in the streets of D.C., secluded from crime and violence. It was a safe place, this town; secluded from normal, everyday folks. It was a hidden secret; a privileged location, especially for the elite crowd.

"Thank you baby," I said. I reached over and grabbed his hand. I squeezed it tightly. "Thank you," I repeated.

As Garrett cruised down the street, I noticed there was one lane coming into town and another lane heading out. I stared out the car window to see couples seated in and around outdoor tables of restaurants: Italian, American, Japanese and other authentic cuisines. The smell of slow baked, fresh Italian bread lingered in the air.

There were men dressed in suits sitting outside the wine and cigar bars. Other men were dressed casually in slacks. Wine in one hand, and a cigar in the other. I wonder what their topics of discussions were? Hmmm ... puff, puff ... I could see the smoke from their cigars escaping into the air. I could see them sipping, indulging themselves with their fine wines.

Class, elegance and prestige, all of that came to mind. I could no longer hear the sounds of music through the car speakers. Instead, I heard the sound of jazz. Yeah, this was one "jazzy" little town.

How could I expect any less from Garrett? Everything was top notch with him.

"Thanks sweetheart, this is lovely" I said.

"Anything for you Luv," Garrett replied. He pulled the car into the parking lot. There was a parking attendant there dressed in a black suit. Garrett walked over to my car door to open it. As we walked up to the restaurant door, I could feel the energy from inside protruding outdoors.

Wow. I thought. I was really feeling the ambiance of the place ... nice! I looked around at the crowd of people. The majority were Caucasian couples; some tables had ladies only, and a few tables had African Americans. That restaurant was really packed. We barely got a seat that night. There was a piano in the corner, but we had already missed the night's entertainment. The lights were very dim.

The candles lit the round tables covered with white tablecloths. The kitchen was open; anyone could see the chefs preparing the food. I liked that, I liked it a lot! The chefs wore their tall white chef's hats. The waitresses were dressed in black and white.

"Follow me, right this way to your table." The hostess said. She ushered us to follow her.

We both were starving. It was written all over our faces, even in our eyes. Maybe that's why we both were behaving like crabs earlier, we were hungry man! I was typically the one known for my "Inspector Gadget" tactics, so for Garrett to pull this "fast one" on me was definitely a total surprise.

"Luv, it was so hard riding in that car in total silence with you." He said. "I wanted to crack up so badly. I was in stitches! I wanted you to think I was really upset with you so this would come as a complete surprise."

"Yeah, it is rather hard pulling the wool over my eyes." I replied. "You got me, you got me man. Garrett, I couldn't have asked for a better surprise babe." Our waitress came over to our table to check in on us. We had devoured the food that had been on our plates. We had a little bit of everything. I ordered a nice steak and Garrett ordered everything except the "kitchen sink."

"May I take those out of your way," our waitress said. Garrett leaned forward and whispered in her ear.

"Garrett, you better not be up to any of your tricks." I warned him.

Yep, sure enough Garrett was up to his tricks! The waitress returned with our dessert. Of course mine had a birthday candle in it.

"You are something else Garrett." I said. We were both stuffed. We sat there for a minute after dinner just having casual conversation.

"So how is the family doing?" I asked. Garrett was a man who loved his family deeply.

"Everybody is good Luv," he replied.

Stomachs stuffed, Garrett paid the bill and we were ready to head home to his place. The drive back to D.C. seemed to take forever. We both were tired and exhausted. I was ready to peel off the exhaustion of my long day by taking a nice, warm shower. I couldn't wait to let the water hit my aching body.

I walked into Garrett's master bathroom to find Garrett's favorite picture of me framed on the counter top.

"How sweet babe," I told him. "You didn't have to pull it out from underneath the sink babe."

"Girl you are so crazy," he replied.

Yeah, I ain't crazy one bit. I said to myself.

I don't know where Garrett and I suddenly got this burst of energy, but it was "on and popping" in that bedroom. The very first touch sent waves through my entire body. The anticipation of what was coming next made chills shoot through my spine.

"I missed you Luv," Garrett said.

"Don't tell me, show me just how much you missed me baby," I said.

Why on earth did I say that? Garrett almost broke his back showing me how much he had missed me that

night. The lovemaking was passionate. The strokes were
deep. The kisses to my neck, stomach and thighs were
soft and gentle. We looked into each other's eyes with
each kiss. The kisses were slow and wet. We both
attempted to satisfy each other's longing until we
couldn't take anymore.

That night, not only did "the neighbors know our
names," but the whole damn subdivision knew it! It was
already morning by the time we finished making love.
Hours later after I awoke from a deep sleep rolling out of
bed, I stumbled to my feet to be stopped dead in my
tracks! I glanced down at the floor to find Garrett's gun
in its holster.

32

Hurt So Bad

Blah, blah, blah ... sure, Garrett was wonderful and great. But what did he do to hurt me so deeply? What did he do to mess up this bliss between the two of us? These were the questions I found myself asking. I began to reminisce about our humble beginnings. I found myself reflecting back on our relationship when it was in its early stages. I'm not so sure it was what Garrett *did*, but more of reality was finally setting in of what he did *not* do!

Despite the problems we were facing in our relationship, Garrett and I persevered. We had a bond nonetheless. The signs however at that point, I would have to be a complete fool to ignore. The length of time between calls being returned grew longer. Fewer calls were being initiated by Garrett. The arguments became more intense fueled by my fears of his possible infidelity.

Promises after promises, broken! Bible studies at night? No more, I began finding myself studying and praying alone. What was happening, what was going on ...? The suspicion came. The insecurity began to surface and engulf me.

Garrett once said to me during one of our heated arguments, "Summer, I lost one good woman. I don't want to lose another!"

I felt the sincerity within his words and I also felt the pain when he spoke those words to me. Garrett had shared the story with me about the years of infidelity to his ex-wife; she finally had enough of him staying away for days at a time, and left him. The cheating and only God knows what else had become more than she could bear anymore.

"One day I came home and the house had been packed and emptied," Garrett told me. "My wife was gone. There was nothing I could do to get her back... I tried everything and I mean everything to get her back, nothing worked." I could hear the sincerity in his voice.

When a woman's had enough! There's nothing, and I mean absolutely n-o-t-h-i-n-g you can do about it! Perhaps, Garrett had come to the realization that he was following the same path he had years before. He wasn't ready for a good woman like me. He wasn't ready to settle down as he had previously thought....

Summer, open your eyes if this man wants you he would make a way, I thought. Garrett didn't want to commit. *'Love' is an action word.* Garrett was not in love. *He may have loved you in the beginning, but no more,* I convinced myself. At forty-two, Garrett still wasn't there yet. Garrett, lost one good woman because he couldn't stop running the streets and truth be told, he wasn't done running the streets.

I listened to his confessions and kept my thoughts and opinions to myself. Like they say, "*life goes on*," and there are "*plenty of fish in the sea.*" Easier said than done. You can't make anyone love you, can you? Nah, you really can't. You're lying to yourself if you think you can; especially, someone who is set in their ways.

In my mind, I literally envisioned brushing myself off feeling like I'm up again … *Yeah, I can do this.* Like a boxer in a ring, jumping up and down pumped up from the adrenaline for the next big round of fight. It was time to wipe away the tears. He wasn't crying over me. *Why should I shed another wet tear over him?* I thought. He was simply hiding behind his job as a comfortable excuse not to commit. He wasn't fooling me, Summer.

33

Just Fine

$\mathscr{J}$ suppose the women were already trying to warn me that Garrett was a "ladies' man." Garrett and I had gone to a "new joint" that opened in the city. It was a storefront lounge; a nice intimate spot, to meet up with friends and socialize. We had gone there to meet up with Garrett's friends and "just chill." Of the friends, some included females. Females who were dying to fill my ears the minute Garrett walked away to buy drinks.

"So where are you from?" one asked as she looked over at me with a wicked grin.

"Garrett is always bringing up a new lady friend," the other female said. They all chuckled and laughed aloud.

It was my first encounter with "City" women. I had heard time and time again from men how ruthless and cut-throat they were. Yes, I had heard through the grapevine that they were straight up crazy! Not to be confused, crazy with a "C" and not a "K" for funny! And how they wouldn't dare to think twice about cutting you in a heartbeat.

But I was from the "dirty south" and my looks were not to be deceived either. I was very capable of defending myself in an event of an attack. I wasn't intimidated, nor was I afraid. I could get down with the best of them despite my petite size.

I know they were just looking out for me ... the women simply felt obliged to inform me. It was part of the "sisterhood" right? I think not, those witches just wanted to cause some damn rift between us. If they were truly concerned, something more appropriate would have been: "Garrett is cool and all, but he has a lot of female friends be careful girl." That's if they were truly doing their "sisterhood duty." And it would have been later for all of that extra giggling and shit, right? Right!

I never mentioned to Garrett upon his return nor after we departed, about their complete disrespect towards him and for me, for that matter. The ex-wife packing the house and leaving for good had told me all I needed to know. Reality was, the ex-wife wasn't enough to make Garrett change his whorish ways and neither was I! He wasn't in his twenties or thirties anymore. No, Garrett was now in his forties and he wasn't ready for a commitment again. At least, not with me!

Obviously, Garrett needed much more. More than I, Summer could give him as his woman. I had already begun to see a pattern in some men. Men especially who had so graciously crossed my path. There was something that had become very apparent, very clear to me. Some men were frightened when disagreements surfaced; however, those were the times when your love was tested the most. Those times were your season of "growing pains." Just as teenage boys grow into manhood by experiencing pain throughout their bones, the pain was sure to come with new relationships as they grow and mature.

There it was already, Garrett was ready to leave me. We had our faith, we had our love … wasn't that enough! At forty plus, Garrett wasn't ready to become accountable for his actions again. He could travel back and forth to Virginia, New York and anywhere else at any time without worrying about a woman back at home nagging, questioning him about his whereabouts.

What was going to happen when he became old? Who was going to care for Garrett then? Sure good women, heck great women aren't a rare find in D.C. or anywhere else. But would Garrett be blessed to meet another Summer? That's what I wanted to know Garrett, "Mr. I'm living the single life?"

Reality was, the chances were far greater for a man to meet a great woman than a woman to meet a great man. Obviously Garrett knew this … Lord knows I tried more than I cared to remember to keep our love alive … to keep the blood flowing. Garrett didn't care if another man came and swept me off of my feet. Was I supposed to patiently wait for him to rescue me from the life of singlehood?

He just wasn't ready, I got it. And I got it loud and clear. Garrett just wasn't ready! Did it hurt any less, of course not! It actually cut me "razor sharp" but I had to respect him for not putting me through what I'm sure his ex-wife endured.

I remember a conversation I once had with a very close male friend.

Corey said to me, "Summer, if you only saw the look I saw in my wife's face after I told her that I cheated on her." I could see the lump in his throat as he tried to swallow up the pain still there. He continued, "The hurt, the pain I saw in her eyes ... I will never forget."

Corey went on to say, "And Summer I had a great wife, we had a good marriage! I had no excuse at all to cheat."

"Corey, was she worth it?" I asked him.

"Hell no, Summer you already knew the answer to that one," he said.

"It's never worth it!" we both answered at the same time.

"I did it because I wanted what I saw, period." he said.

"I threw away a great marriage for a one night stand," he told me.

I just sat there as I held my friend's head in my lap. The pain after so many years was relevant; it still mattered, and could be felt so deeply.

"Well, how did she find out?" I asked.

"Because we had such a bond, I couldn't look at her without her seeing that I had already defiled our marriage," he said. "I had to come clean, I just had to."

I felt bad for him because I knew deep down Corey was a good man. Unfortunately, he like countless others couldn't control the wrong head! Reality was … Corey really just needed to clear his own conscious. Who did he think he was fooling?

That was really the truth of the matter.

"I can honestly say with happiness God blessed her with a great new husband," he said. "She has a great man, she's happy again," he told me.

But Corey wasn't happy. He was searching for something he once had in the great wife he threw away for a stupid challenge. A challenge to himself to prove he still had it! But he didn't still have it and neither did Garrett.

Neither one had what countless single people envy; someone who truly has your back one hundred percent. A lifetime partner, period!

Obviously Summer, this was far greater and much bigger than just you! Apparently it's not always about what the man or the woman isn't doing right. It's more about the person's cheating, selfish desires, of their own lust and lack of integrity. Often times, you think you are ready for something because it looks so good and promising then, reality slams the door right in your face! BAM!

Summer, you must learn to let those doors slam and lock them from the inside! I told myself. Don't allow those thieves to come in and rob you of your happiness! You were "just fine" before the robbers came. And you will be "just fine" when their asses leave to rob their next victim!

34

Locked Up

I found myself behind a steel door. Early on in our courtship, Garrett initiated the idea of marriage. He spoke of how his friends were teasing him, making bets that he and I "would be married within a year of knowing each other." Guess all bets were off now, huh Garrett?

Look where we are now; far removed, yet so close within our hearts. At that point, maybe it was for the best. I wish someone had told my heart that! Somebody, anybody! There was nothing funny at all to me. It wasn't a laughing matter, getting your heart handed back to you.

"Laughing at life sometimes is the best therapy to keep yourself from crying!" I said.

Garrett realized he needed to be thrown back into the "fiery furnace." There was more refinement needed. There I was placing the blame all on Garrett. Truth be told, I had some fine tuning that was needed also "Ms. I could do no wrong Summer."

The Most Loved

35

King and Queen

I heard stories about Garrett's neighborhood friends. I was excited to one day possibly meet the "Da Bronx" friends of Garrett. Did our problems go away? No, they did not. We just kept pushing forward, uncertain exactly, of the direction we were heading.

It was late summer when I flew up to D.C. to spend some quality time with Garrett. New York City was Garrett's hometown and it was a place I had always dreamed of visiting. Garrett and I had conversations about me visiting his family and friends. He always spoke so fondly of them all.

I always felt that New York was too much city for this southern girl. The northern states I always avoided due to the horrible stories I heard from Richard's family up north. On this day however, Summer had finally arrived! The big "city of dreams!" And the man making it all possible was a man I adored, my baby, Garrett.

One of Garrett's closest friends, Jon, had been there in D.C. visiting with him from New York that week. It had been a week of adventure; amusement parks, and whatever else men do! My flight arrived in D.C. the night before our scheduled road trip to New York. I was so happy and excited to see my baby!

Jon was a real cool guy.

"I hope Jon hadn't heard us from the basement doing the nasty." I laughed as I told Garrett to quiet it down some!

Poor Jon, I thought. Maybe he was playing music and couldn't hear us on the second floor. Garrett's home had three levels and a basement. I honestly didn't see how it was possible for Jon not to hear, but that's what I had hoped.

The lovemaking was heartfelt. Wild and crazy would have been an understatement on that night. Oh my! I don't think either of us knew we were so limber.

"This is it Summer," Garrett said to me as I stared down over him. Garrett assured me, that he wanted no one but me.

"It was going to be just the two of us from that night forward," he said. And into a deep sleep we both fell. I don't know if he was speaking from the heart, or because he was sprung that night!

The next morning arrived and we were "on the road again." The music blared through the sound system of his Benz. It was humorous to me as I listened to forty something year old men singing along to a young rap kid's cd.

Who was I kidding? This young kid was what was happening ... he was hot on the scene in the music industry! A mixture of rap along with singing; yeah, I could dig it! I got it. I knew. Garrett just wanted to be successful!

In the front passenger seat of Garrett's S-class Mercedes; the soft leather seats cuddled my small frame as if I were a newborn in a mother's arm. We were the King and Queen on the road. The ride was smooth; just as it would be if we were sailing the calm waters of the ocean. Garrett's Mercedes was a beast on the highway. It was huge ... a great look for "Mr. all I want to be is successful!"

Garrett and I both looked the part of success. We were good looking, smart, well put together. Notice I said "looked the part." Garrett and I were both far from where we wanted to be in life. Although, I would have been content, with just someone to love me, Garrett needed so much more as a single man living in D.C.

The drive was hours long. I looked out of the window at the big differences the north was from the south. Concrete everywhere! "Concrete jungle" was our first destination. Jersey City. I saw no green lawns, beaches, or palm trees. No, this was definitely not Florida. It wasn't even Georgia for that matter. It was "Jerseeeey!"

I looked around as we entered Jersey City. This was a distant land compared to my "home sweet home" in Florida. People walked the streets with no apparent place to go, just walking. A gang of guys hanging outside of the front steps of homes. Liquor and store fronts everywhere we turned. No, I was missing absolutely nothing in Jersey City. This was indeed, a different animal!

Sure, I felt uncomfortable in this environment which made me very nervous, but I was with Garrett. Being with him made everything okay! He would never allow anything at all to happen to me. I loved Garrett and wouldn't have wanted to be anywhere else at that moment. Okay, I lied ... maybe the Bahamas, but I was still happy!

Jon was in a deep sleep in the back seat. He slept almost the entire ride up. Garrett was my tour guide and I wouldn't have had it any other way. I fought back tears as I erased thoughts that this may never happen again for Garrett and I. I shook it off quickly and reminded myself ...

Summer live for the moment. Whatever time Garrett and I had left on this ride … for now, I just wanted to ride it out and enjoy.

The Most Loved

36

Blood Is Thick

*G*arrett was always a true gentleman. He opened my car door as we arrived at his uncle's house in Jersey.

"Thanks sweetie, you are such a gentleman." I told him.

"Luv, I didn't always open the car doors for women," he said. "It was actually something I learned to do over time as a man," he told me.

"Well, I thank you for the lesson learned" I said. Along went a kiss from my lips to his.

Garrett wanted to stop in New Jersey en route to New York. His favorite uncle, "Earl" lived there along with his wife Loretta. Most members in Garrett's family had a problem with Uncle Earl because of his heavy drinking. Was Garrett amongst the group of haters? Of course not, he was crazy about his Uncle Earl. I was eager to meet anyone Garrett loved and cared for and Uncle Earl was at the top of the list.

Meeting Uncle Earl, I could see why Garrett was so fond of him. Garrett had the same humor as his uncle. Sometimes, I wondered if Garrett wasn't a heavy drinker himself. Hmmm .... I can't explain it ... I never saw any real signs, but my gut told me there was much I hadn't learned about Garrett's past or present life.

"Summer, this is Uncle Earl," Garrett said.

"It's a pleasure to meet you, I've heard so much about you," I told him.

"Don't believe anything of what you've heard," he said. Uncle Earl had been in his detached garage along the back of the driveway when we walked up on him.

I had never seen anything like that before. Uncle Earl had it "hooked" up in that garage. I'm talking a refrigerator, his music, and boy did he have a collection of some good music blaring, real music! There was no mistaking it, this was Uncle Earl's "man cave."

"Hey man," Uncle Earl said to Jon.

"What up Uncle Earl," Jon replied.

Garrett's Uncle Earl and his Aunt Loretta were so warm and inviting. I fell in love with them instantly. It felt as though I was back home in the south. Aunt Loretta was my just type of lady. She had a fish fry going on up in that kitchen! Little did any of them know that was right up my alley. A fish fry? Oooo wee! I was ready to roll up my sleeves and dig in. Hot fish, mustard, ketchup, white bread and yes Lord, some hot sauce. Yum yum!

Yes sir, yes sir. I was lovin' me some Jersey folks up there that day! Good southern hospitality right in Jersey City.

"Did you get enough to eat Luv?" Garrett asked.

"Yes sweetie, I'm good." I replied.

Jon was with us.

"This is some good fish," Jon said. I could tell that this wasn't Jon's first time being in their home. But Jon was ready to get back home to his own family. He had already been away from his wife and son a week while there visiting with Garrett on vacation. It was time we got him back home.

After eating and watching a little television, Garrett and I nodded off on one another a few times.

"Hey man, you ready to roll," Jon said. Garrett looked over at Jon.

"Yeah man, we can get ready to head out," he said.

"It was such a pleasure meeting you guys," I told Uncle Earl and Aunt Loretta.

"We look forward to seeing you again," they said.

"You can count on it," I replied. "I sincerely appreciate your hospitality, thank you" I told them both.

As we prepared to leave, one of Garrett's cousins stopped through.

"Hey, what's up," he said.

"Hey, how are you?" I asked.

"I hear you are from Florida," Randy said.

"Yep, that would be me," I told him.

"Garrett and I are gonna have to take a road trip," he said.

"Come on," I said.

"Bet, bet. We are definitely coming down," he assured me.

"Sure thing," I told him.

It was quite refreshing to meet a family who welcomed you. I didn't have to feel people staring at me or asking me stupid questions. I was happy that I didn't have to go through an interrogation either. *If only more people were more welcoming and honestly give people an opportunity to feel comfortable.* I thought.

I wished more people would learn to treat strangers like family, instead of like strangers. "Sometimes God sends angels who are entertained unaware," and sometimes He sends just regular folk who have the love of God within them, like me … Summer!

37

City Of Dreams

cross the George Washington Bridge from New Jersey and into "The City" we went. *The Big Apple. The City of Dreams.* Traffic was everywhere! Car after car, after car.

"Wow, do they really charge this much just to enter the city? Over eight dollars baby?" I asked.

"Yes Luv, it's expensive huh?" He said.

"Unbelievable … George Washington on the one dollar bill and then he takes it right back on the bridge named after him," I said. We all chuckled.

"Luv look," Garrett said. He was pointing out towards the Hudson River.

"Oh yeah, that's where the plane landed in the river," I said.

"Yep, right between New Jersey and New York," he replied.

"I know it was US Airways Flight 1549," I told him. I looked out in amazement. Actually, I was more like gawking at that point.

"A lot has changed throughout the city," Garrett said. "I want to take you by ground zero Luv," he said. It was so unreal that day—to witness where the tragedy of 9/11 took place.

I'm sure all Americans can remember, no matter how many years pass, the exact place and what they were doing when the Twin Towers fell. The day 9/11 occurred; the attack on America. How dare those sons of evil invade our nation in our "City of Dreams!" They created a nightmare that America would never wake up from.

It was such a wet, rainy day as we made our way through the area. At the time, we couldn't get very close to ground zero. Construction was underway and there were metal fences all around. The rain would not let up. Garrett actually slowed down the speed of his driving some. Earlier, I thought we were on a damn rollercoaster ride the way he weaved in and out of traffic. I don't know how he was able to do that maneuvering in that big ass car!

As the down pour finally cleared the skies, Garrett accelerated his speed trying to make it through the heavy traffic. I looked in the back seat.

"Jon, my buddy ole' pal, you sure you don't want to get up front in the passenger seat?" I asked. Jon looked up and smiled at me.

"You got it Summer," he said.

"No the heck I don't," I told him. You'd swear Garrett had officially become the next NASCAR driver that day.

Looking out of the window, I saw the entrances to the subway stations. The taxi cabs were passing one after the other; just as you see in all of the television series and in movies. It was true, taxis were everywhere in New York City! The streets were full of people everywhere too!

"Wow, so this is New York," I said. My dreams were coming true! I had finally made it to New York.

Yankee Stadium, Central Park. Garrett made it a point to take me through each of the five boroughs of New York: Manhattan, Brooklyn, the Bronx, Queens (Jamaica) and Staten Island were all the boroughs of NYC.

I was head over heels in love with some New York City. There was some big event that was going on at Yankee Stadium and that made traffic worse. I looked over out of Garrett's driver side mirror and saw he had some type of NYC decal for law enforcement. Hell, I didn't know Garrett was Jamaican. This man had five damn jobs. How in the heck did he have authority all the way in NYC?

Somehow, we finally managed to get Jon back to his family in Brooklyn. At some point I just lost track of where we were anymore. No, I was too amazed at what my eyes were taking in to pay attention to anything else.

We socialized for a minute with Jon's wife Lisa. She was good people. I liked her. She seemed friendly enough. Jon was blessed with a nice family; pretty wife and handsome son. I see why he was anxious to get back to them. *If only Garrett could have wanted the same.* I thought.

I guess what works for one man, doesn't quite work for the other. Sure, like most couples—I'm sure Jon and Lisa have had their share of problems, but they are still together ... right? At the end of the day, isn't that what matters most?

Lights, lights and more lights ... People at every turn—Times Square was what Garrett had in mind for me! He wanted me in the center of it all. Oh, Garrett spared no expense–he had indeed gone *all* out! It was hundreds of dollars per night for the hotel we stayed in and the room wasn't as large as some closets. From the decor and the furnishings, this was a very elegant place.

Not to mention the executive guests I noticed there, can you say "upscale?"

Yes indeed, I was impressed, but Garrett didn't have to impress me. Everyone made me out as this "high maintenance queen" but that wasn't who I was. Absolutely, I loved the finer things in life, but I wasn't for a moment trying to break Garrett's pocket no matter how deep they were. I loved him for him, nothing more and nothing less … for him!

As tired as Garrett and I were, it didn't stop us from wanting each other so badly! We mustered up strength to pleasure, please and tease each other that night. It was greeeeat just as it always had been each time before. Our bodies were in rhythm with one another the same as our hearts.

The morning came way too early for us. The rain was still coming down, but was beginning to lighten up a bit.

"Good morning Luv," Garrett said.

"Morning babe," I said.

"We are going to pick up my older brother," he told me. "He's getting married, we have to do our fitting today for our tuxedos while I'm up here."

I met several of Garrett's brothers and a few of his very close friends while we were there. Man, I have never met so many cool guys at one time. They were cool as hell! It was like dealing with my own brothers. We hit it off great from the very start. We went through the city making stops picking up two of Garrett's brothers; Ronnie, Bobby and his friend Ricky. Nah, I'm just teasing! Seriously, we picked up Tommy, Derrick and Tim.

"Summer, which tux you like best?" Tommy asked.

Honestly, I didn't like any of those ugly tuxedos. If I had to choose though, well again—I didn't like any of them. They all knew those suits sucked.

"Girl, those are some bad heels you got on there," Derrick said.

'Thanks," I replied.

"Where down south are you from?" Tommy asked.

"Dang, is my accent that obvious?" I asked.

They all looked at me and said "Yeah!"

I laughed and said, "Yeah, I suppose it is!"

"It's all good," Derrick assured me.

Tommy told the owner that he needed to do more looking around before he made a decision. We all were thankful for that one. Instead of driving, we walked the streets of NYC. Thank God we didn't have a whole lot of walking to do. After all, I was wearing heels.

We went to one other tuxedo place that Tommy's fiancé recommended. Tim and I stood around chit chatting. He was a great guy. I really liked his personality. He was a good dude. I could tell. Man, I wished there were more brothers like those fellas in Florida. Instead of

"B—ch" this and "Whore" that! The majority, have no respect at all for women. I'm not saying all, but damn near eighty percent all!

Garrett went back to get the car so we could head on our way. Meanwhile, Derrick decided he was hungry and would go get him some pizza. We waited around for a while and Derrick had not returned. Garrett decided to go look to see where Derrick had run off to. He finally came dancing along. Meanwhile, Garrett hadn't returned from looking for him.

We stood beside the car and shot the breeze. Derrick began to step in a dance motion; hands in sync with his feet. I copied his movement and duplicated the step. We were cutting up along the sidewalk wilding out until Garrett came along and killed the show. He had this "let's roll" look on his face. We cracked up in laughter! Yeah, Derrick was cool as hell. We both were acting a fool having fun on the sidewalks of New York, New York.

One by one, we began making our drop off stops.

"Hey Summer, it was a pleasure meeting you," Derrick said.

"Likewise, likewise," I replied.

"Congrats on your wedding Tommy," I said as we dropped him off.

"Yep thanks, nice meeting you," Tommy said. "What's your name again?" he asked.

"Summer," I replied.

"Yeah, nice meeting you Summer," he said.

Tim was our last drop off. Garrett got out of the car this time when he dropped his friend Tim off.

"Summer, it was a pleasure and I do mean a pleasure meeting you," Tim said. "I know I will be seeing you again," he assured me. Garrett and Tim went to the back of the car.

In the most respectful manner, Tim was trying to reassure me that I was a keeper. At least that's the way I took it. Possibly even that he thought Garrett and I had a promising future. Reminiscing of where it all began, it all seemed like a dream anymore.

"Luv, you hungry?" Garrett asked.

"You know I'm always hungry," I said. Manhattan was where Garrett and I were headed. It was time for some good southern food before we traveled back to

D.C. I was taking all of New York in and really digging it as I looked around my surroundings.

Garrett brushed the Benz alongside the curb as we pulled up to the storefront. I lifted up my head to smile as an older women passed by. Our eyes locked and I gave her my warm southern smile. The woman's lips moved uttering something ... through the window.

"Do you have change for a hundred?" she asked. Before I could even open my door completely, Garrett jumped out of the car and over to the passenger door.

"Hey, hey, hey—come here," Garrett said. His New York accent was extremely heavy as he called her out. "Now you know you don't have a hundred dollars yourself, you hungry?" He asked the old woman. "Luv, I'll be right back," he said. Garrett ushered me along to go inside the restaurant without him.

"Luv, rule of thumb ... that old woman was going to snatch your wallet the minute it was visible," he said. "You can't bring that southern girl hospitality up here with you Luv. These people are ruthless. Every man is out to get something," he told me. Garrett had his way of politely scolding me that day! Regardless of this little encounter I was still in love with NYC, you can believe that!

Collard greens, corn bread, BBQ chicken, you name it and Garrett and I ate it. Our meal must have come up to sixty dollars or more with tip. My mouth dropped to the floor.

"Do you know we could have eaten the same meal in Florida for less than twenty bucks baby," I told him. I was shocked at the price.

"Luv, we are in Manhattan you are going to pay hefty bucks here," he said. Again, we pigged out. We ate up everything. I don't know where I put all that food, but I was hanging right in there with Garrett.

On our drive from New York, there was something different about Garrett. I don't know if it was exhaustion from all of the driving, but he appeared distant. It had been a very busy weekend and he had a lot of preparation to do. Entertaining Jon the entire week and then, I came up.

Either way, I couldn't shake that feeling of separation between us. I rested Garrett's right hand on my thigh as he drove. He wasn't very responsive. I couldn't call it. I really didn't know what was going through his mind. Distance between us reared its ugly little head once again. There was just no escaping it where Garrett was concerned.

38

A Bond Not Easily Broken

"*Are you threatening me Garrett?*" I asked.

"No Luv, I'm not threatening you," he said.

From Garrett's reaction, it was apparent that my pregnancy was not one of deliberate intention. Then how? I thought. How was I holding a pregnancy test which read "positive?"

I rubbed my hands across my forehead. The tension would not go away! What was going on in that man's head? Who was he? I felt as if I didn't know him anymore. What was happening? Why had this happened to me? Make it go away. I just wanted it all to go away!

I looked across the huge lake imaging myself swimming across it—butt ass naked. "I'm losing my mind," I said. You promised yourself that you would never let anyone break you down the way Ray did ever again Summer! Don't you remember Summer, you promised! My inner voice, my spirit wouldn't allow me to fall again. Remembering what I endured with Ray and how I thought I could never love again after he had hurt me so deep! Yet, I also thought I could never love again after Richard either.

Can't you see Summer ... you can heal. You can move on ... all it takes is time! Time is your best friend. Time has all the answers you need in life. It delivers. It restores. It forgives. Just be patient and give it time Summer. I know it's raining cats and dogs right now, but this too shall pass. Have faith, believe, and trust Summer! Trust God, not man! Look through God's eyes.

I wiped my tears. It was time I faced the reality of my dilemma. I didn't make any more calls to Garrett. I needed to give the situation a few days to calm itself. Yeah, that's exactly what I needed to do. I had been known to prematurely jump to assumptions at times. Maybe I just needed to give Garrett some space. After all, it was now obvious that *this news* was a complete shock to us *both*.

My keys fell from my hands as I tried to open my car door. My hands were shaking nervously from my nervous system being turned upside down. I took a minute to inhale and exhale. I stood there for a solid minute and tried again.

My best friend, London, was always my voice of reason. My cellular phone in hand as the rings rang out ...

" London," I cried.

"Summer, what on earth is wrong sweetie?" she asked. I was crying so hard I could barely get the words out!

"I need you London," I said. "I feel as if I have no one to turn to," I told her. Disappointment consumed me as I told London about my predicament.

"I'm pregnant."

"Oh sweetie, stop crying it is going to be okay," she said. London reassured me that I had her full support.

"Sweetie, please tell me what's going on?" she asked. London knew everything there was to know about my relationship with the *man of my dreams*.

She wasn't just any female. No, she was the big sister that I never had. She wouldn't allow anyone to hurt me if it were in her control. She loved me. She was my biggest cheerleader. She believed in me. Anything that I verbalized that I wanted to do, London was right there one hundred percent.

She knew of Garrett and my hopes of a future together. In addition, she was also aware that things started to take a turn for the worse in our relationship as well. The continuous conversations with London of how I began to see that Garrett's job in Secret Service and law enforcement along with the long distance made me doubt if our love would endure. All of that was a clue to London why I was crying.

"What did Garrett say about you being pregnant?" She asked. London was careful to tread lightly with her words. She could tell that I was in a sensitive and very emotional state.

"I haven't heard one word from Garrett after the doctor confirmed that I was a month pregnant," I told her.

"Forget him, we can take care of this baby by ourselves," she said. "You can do this girl, you are a strong woman."

"I know, I know London, but financially I am already struggling and the baby daddy drama that I already go through with Jaden's father has been a living hell. I don't want to have a baby out of wedlock and be a single mother. London, I know you love me and I know you are pro-life. I don't want to cheat this child of having a father and I can't bear seeing my child suffer." I told her.

I quickly dismissed London's suggestions.

"Summer, you can do this," she reinforced. Finally feeling as if I could possibly do it! I convinced myself there must be a reason this happened—we were so careful. God must want this!

Ring, ring, ring, ring, ring ... "Hello, you have reached my voice mail. Please do leave the pertinent contact information and your call will be returned … *beep*." I had reached Garrett's voice mail greeting.

"Garrett, this is Summer, please give me a call. I haven't heard from you at all. I have decided I am keeping this child whether you want to be a part of this child's life or not," I said. The call ended. I couldn't hang the phone up completely before Garrett was blowing my phone up.

"Oh now you can call me, you jackass." I said as I looked at the phone seeing his name on the caller ID. I had been anticipating what Garrett was going to say. I grasped on to every sound within the earpiece waiting for Garrett to speak. His voice was low and his words slow ... I could feel a scared little boy confused who did not know where to go, where to turn ... a little boy needing guidance ... he needed any source of direction to make the right decision. Garrett was terrified, we *both* were!

How could this be? We were two adults. Yes, we were performing adult behavior, but this wasn't supposed to happen! We were so *very* careful! We were careful! Protection was used each and *every* time.

"Summer, you don't want to do this," Garrett said. His job was to try to convince me to change my mind.

"Garrett, whether you decide to be a part of this child's life or not I am keeping my baby," I said.

"Summer, I don't want any kids," he said. "I don't want kids ...."

I screamed, "This isn't about you Garrett! This is *my* body and *my* choice," I told him.

"Do you think by you having this child this is going to keep me?" He asked.

I thought I would blow a fuse at that moment! I had reached my boiling point! I was a tea kettle and I was ready to explode with steam!

"Don't flatter yourself asshole," I snapped at him.

"I don't need to hold on to *you* or *any* other man for that matter," I told him. "This child is a part of me. Do you hear me Garrett? A part of *me*!" I yelled.

I was so upset that I began to cry uncontrollably.

"You just don't know what this week has been like for me," I cried. "It's been a living hell. You have had the luxury of doing a complete disappearing act." I barked at him.

"You will have this baby without my help Summer," he told me.

"Well, that's your decision Garrett not mine," I told him.

I was absolutely disgusted at him. Garrett and I hung up the telephone with not much else said between the two of us. I was going to have this baby whether I had to take care of it alone or not. I was having it. I had finally felt my help coming from the Lord. I dried my tears.

I was making the right decision. Children are a blessing. I *am* making the right decision and then, that ugly, wicked and evil devil came to cast doubt! He had a job to do which was to "kill, steal and destroy." And the devil wanted my baby *dead*! Why on earth did I doubt the Lord's ability to care for me and my child? God had always remained faithful in His promises. God was a promise keeper!

Whatever my decision … one thing was certain; our lives would never be the same! We would forever share "a bond not easily broken."

The Most Loved

39

You Have The Rights

*U*nfortunately, one of my characteristics was order, and a planned itinerary. Everything must be in place beforehand. Spontaneity wasn't in my cards....

I had to think of a strategy for how I would make this all happen for me and my children. Not to forget that whatever my decision was, it would affect Jaden. Jaden had suffered enough already. The divorce shattered my baby. How on earth was I going to make it all work out for good, Lord?

Reality struck me like a bolt of "Tampa Bay lightning" ... single, unwed, no health insurance, new job and less pay thanks to "white collar America." One of the largest corporations in the country, and yet my job had been outsourced overseas. All of my hard work and dedication for a tired ass compensation package! Only to have to train the very people who were taking over my job. Total nonsense! I was so disgusted.

Let me see ... there would be prenatal expenses, doctor's visits. And then, the delivery and any additional hospital expenses would have to be taken care of by *me* alone. Wow, not to mention all of the other expenses associated with a newborn. Overwhelmed wasn't quite the word I was searching for. It was more like "defeated." I felt totally defeated.

Could I really take the chance of Garrett coming around later? Did I truly know who I was dealing with? Could Garrett be a good father? This *love saga* all happened so very fast. Did I really know the type of man Garrett would have been to my child in the long run?

"Garrett, this is Summer," I said. My voice was soft and faint. I had convinced myself of all the reasons I couldn't have the baby. But what I should have done was thought of all of the joy Jaden brought to my life and how he had always given me reason to go on, *purpose*!

As a mother, it was my job to protect my unborn child. I should have considered how *strong* I was instead of allowing my weakness to defeat me.

"I have made the decision to not have this child," I said. "It has nothing to do with *you*, but my own personal decision." I told him. I had announced my final decision! I was in such a denial state of mind. Why was I lying to *myself* and to *Garrett*? My decision had *everything* to do with him!

In the end, wasn't this exactly what Garrett wanted? No, it wasn't the house with the white picket fence as Garrett had promised when we first met. Nope, that was not it. And it definitely wasn't for him to love me for a lifetime anymore either.

This entire relationship had gone from bad, to a freakin' *"nightmare on Summer Street"* featuring Summer Covington! My last name should have been "rain" because that was how the sunshine always ended in my life. Somehow, it always ended leaving me drenched in a down pour.

Santos wondered *why* I fled the scene. *Why* I ran away? It was simply just *too good to be true*! Another "Garrett take two" on film, starring "Summer." If only you could have "walked a mile in my shoes" Santos dear. You would be able to comprehend how frightened to death at the mere thought of something so surreal being a true gift for me.

40

Our Love

"Garrett, I can't have the procedure here in Florida," I whispered.

"I will find some clinics in the surrounding area of D.C. and Virginia." He said.

"Summer, I will fly you here and take care of everything. Allow me to do some research and I'll get back with you this week." He reassured me. Oh, now he wanted to be "Mr. Nice Guy" again ... what a complete damn joke!

Deep down inside … yes, I knew that Garrett was like a scared little boy facing a wolf in the woods. In my eyes, Garrett was always strong. He was full of strength with a hearty laugh that could fill any empty room. Today, on this very day ... I saw no such man! What I saw *today* was a vulnerable, terrified young boy! Fact remained, we both were scared lifeless.

As the days passed within the week that followed, anger and resentment began to consume me. How could a *man* who I thought so highly of ... a *man* who I thought was my best friend ... a *man* who touched me deeply within and who lit a spark to light my fire ... how could a *man* cause such a blazing everlasting inferno? How could you do this to me Garrett ... how could you Luv?

41

Dead at My Brother's Hands

The gift of life, ending with *death*! Not on my brother's birthday, how could you Summer? Surely, if my brother ever found out I would be dead at my brother's hands. Although, totally unintentional ... it didn't matter at that point.

It would never have mattered at all to Kurtis. He would kill me! Choke me straight out! I didn't realize it was on his birthday. I honestly didn't know until after the appointment was made. I had to go through with it! Like I said, Kurtis wouldn't hear any of it. He could never find out. Never!

Staff ran from the front of the clinic back to the recovery area. Cries blared from deep within the walls of my soul.

"No, no, noo," I screamed! "My baby, my baby!" Screams and cries were all anyone could hear.

It felt like eternity to everyone there in the clinic. I was convinced that God was punishing me. At that moment He was making me feel every emotion he gave to a human being. I imagine that is what a soul casted down to hell felt like. I had never in my life experienced such torture emotionally and mentally.

The staff rushed anxiously trying to get me removed from the facilities as soon as possible. I had lost my mind. It was apparent to everyone there I had made the *wrong* decision. There were far too many other women who were there awaiting the same fate. This was wrong! This shouldn't be allowed … I was totally convinced that abortion was *wrong* afterwards.

My cries were uncontrollable. There was nothing anyone could do to stop them! It was a mother's pain she bore from losing a child.

Dominic showed up just in time before they decided to throw me out of the clinic. Garrett wired me the money as promised for the procedure and for my hotel reservation. I tried to avoid having the memory of the recovery anywhere where my everyday routine would be. Dominic and I traveled a little ways away from the immediate area where I resided.

"Would you like for me to come up?" Dominic asked.

"No, I'll be ok," I replied. The medicine was slowly wearing off a bit. "I may need you to get me some pain pills," I said.

"Come on let's go eat a nice dinner," Dominic said. "I know how greedy you are, I know you are hungry." he teased me. He actually managed to get a smile out of me.

"Ok, I'll try to eat something," I said.

Dinner was nice. It was actually at one of my favorite steakhouses. Dominic was right. It was what I needed. And what I needed was a dear friend. Dominic and I always had such a strong friendship. It was genuine. The times I needed him the most, he was always there.

"Would you like for me to come up Summer?" He asked. "My little care bear," he teased me.

"Will you stop it silly man," I told him.

Dominic always said I had a heart of gold. He would tell me all of the time that he had never met such a loving and caring woman in all his life. And me knowing Dominic there was no way he could have counted them all! I definitely took that one as a compliment.

"Thank you, but no I prefer to be alone," I told him. "I just need some time and space," I said.

"Totally understandable," he replied. "I'll give you a call tomorrow. Summer, I love you. Please don't hesitate to call me if you need anything, and I mean anything."

"Ok thanks," I said. I gave him a big hug and turned around to head towards the elevator.

The hotel was fabulous. It was nothing less than a four star hotel. As I turned towards the elevator I looked around to see the elegance of the lobby. It was definitely top notch. It was one of my favorites that I occasionally booked whenever I wanted to treat myself to some "me" time. I was tired and I just really needed to be left alone.

Once I entered my room, I went straight to turn the television on. I then went into the bathroom and showered. How I loved four and five star hotels. They always had everything you needed. And anything you didn't have, it was always one phone call away. I went to the bathroom to check myself. I wasn't quite sure what I should have expected from the procedure.

There was absolutely *no* blood, and *no* pain. If only I could have erased the memory of it all away also so easily. Thinking back … the most difficult of it all was the ultrasound procedure. It had been performed to confirm the pregnancy and that everything was normal before they proceeded. It was almost as if the doctor was giving me one last opportunity to exit the grave mistake I was about to make!

I always said I could never imagine or even fathom the thought of my child being murdered. Well guess what? My time had arrived! I was now feeling the pain.

Yet instead, it was me that was "accused, charged, and guilty of the crime of murder!" Summer, a murderer! I killed my *own* child! And it was punishable by "guilt" for the rest of my God given days.

And to think, Garrett never even called afterwards to see if I survived myself! *What would he say Summer?* I mean really! The child was a part of my body. I felt the morning sickness. I was experiencing the weight gain very early. It was me, Summer, experiencing it all. Lock me behind the walls of my soul, the cries of my unborn baby stories that will never unfold ... all because two consenting adults; conducting adult behavior, couldn't say "no" to sex out of wedlock! Pen in hand, ink spilled and it landed on paper:

Don't cry baby ...

Mommy heard your plea …

I didn't want to do it,

But the ultimate decision was left solely on me!

You see, Daddy laid …

But, the dedicated for life part …

He wouldn't play!

I wanted to vanish,

I thought …

This is what you get for being mannish!

I wished I could have escaped …

But, it was far too late.

Don't cry baby ...

Mommy and Daddy will forever be sorry ...

Always wondering what you might have been tomorrow.

For each day that goes by, we live with regret and sorrow.

I wish I could take it all back ...

For in my arms your precious head would lay.

I'm so sorry little one,

Mommy should have protected you that day.

Can you ever forgive us little one,

For the harm we did to you?

Mommy, Daddy ...

I forgive your sin

Loving and forgiving yourselves ...

Is where the healing will begin.

I see your hearts bleed ...

Holding on to possibilities,

You will never be free ...

It's okay to let go of me ...

Mommy and Daddy I accept your plea!

Go now and live your life, be free.

42

Hear My Plea

"Luv, I wanted to call you." Garrett said. "I picked up the phone again and again to say don't do it. I didn't follow through to call you Luv," he told me.

Garrett was now feeling the guilt! *Bullshit*. I thought. *How convenient of him to say that to me now*. I thought. Little did Garrett know, my best friend London wasn't there as she had always been in the past.

London was "pro-life" and didn't agree with my decision at all. Disgusted was how I felt towards Garrett! No, it was Dominic who was actually the one there for me. He was understanding and compassionate; exactly what I needed at a time like that.

I didn't want to fly to D.C. to be near Garrett. In fact, I wanted him as far away from me as possible.

I told Garrett, "I don't blame *you* for the decision was solely on me." Let's face it, had Garrett stepped up as *real* men do in those type of situations ... I would never have considered aborting our child. I know I had responsibility as well. Hell, I was the mother. The child was inside of *me*. I should have protected my unborn child.

If I was disgusted and angry with anyone it should have been at myself, *me* ... Summer! Yeah, *you* Ms. Summer! Whether that man was there or not, it was up to *you* to give your child life. Your excuses were just that, *excuses*! You weren't justified in your decision either. It was selfish! You thought about Summer. It was shallow and just downright selfish. *You can't hide from that mistake Summer... ever, no not never!*

Was it the embarrassment of your sinful shame? My guilty conscious rang loud in my ears over and over again. The rings were almost deafening. Aborting a child is something that would live with me forever in my heart. Hindsight, fully comprehending now ... London warned me, but I didn't listen ... I can't undo it. I can *never* undo it!

There wasn't one single day that I didn't live with the regret of that day. I lost a special part of me. Healing begins with forgiveness. Understanding forgiveness does not mean that you will *ever* forget, but what it does mean is accepting healing. Jesus forgave the men who crucified Him on the cross, forgiving those who were ignorant of their sins, utterly oblivious.

Garrett and I were two well put together individuals, yet in that decision we were "dumb and dumber," the "blind leading the blind!" I had to forgive *Garrett*, I had to forgive *Summer*. The time had finally arrived for us to live life free of guilt, and shame, but instead, in total repentance.

We stood before the court nervous, quiet, humble, and sorrowful as we awaited our sentencing. In our hearts we begged the court for its grace and mercy upon us.

"How do you find the defendants your Honor?" Jesus asked.

"My verdict is: Jesus, *you* have already paid the price for their sins I find them both *innocent*," said I am that I am. "I am the only Judge and Jury in this case ... you all are now dismissed."

The Most Loved

43

Seeds To Bear

$\mathcal{S}$ easons changed—everyone I met wasn't meant to be a mate. Some people came to simply "open up" the container of seeds in preparation. A special someone came to "prepare the ground" for new growth! I didn't pay very close attention in those cases.

Experience should have taught me that it was extremely important when healthy, vibrant gardens are expected, that you "turn over" the top layer of "old" soil. Old soil is equivalent to your ex's in other words. By tilling the ground, you will uncover fresh soil underneath. Once fresh soil has been flipped, you are no longer smothered by your past. You now have the opportunity to come up and breathe fresh air again.

I should have tilled my land often when I experienced bad crops! However, realizing they "all" served a purpose for the end result!

There were people I met who were capable of coming in and immediately sprinkling seeds all over my lawn, garden, or flower bed. Those people were what one would call "seasoned croppers!" They've experienced this process a time or two that I was now experiencing. They had travelled successfully the path upon which I was now attempting to travel.

I should have put on my overalls, stood beside them and learned, learned, learned! Observation was key. There was no need for me to be afraid to ask questions or to be humble in spirit while in their presence. Always listen more attentively than you speak around "seasoned croppers."

Most people we encounter this day and age really have to roll up their sleeves and get downright dirty! Oh, trust me ... they must dig "deep" into the soil before they are able to plant *one* single seed! Why is this? It's called past "roots." Yes, that's right! "Roots" that have been around for so many years, they have grown stubborn and resistant! They are rooted very, very deep in a dark place.

These types of "aged roots" will cause plumbing problems in your household! *Did you hear me*? I said, these type of "roots" cause problems in your household! In your household people! Get rid of those dark roots a.k.a. "your past."

I wanted to move on several times– I thought I was ready for my field to be cultivated so it could finally grow into something beautiful and nutritious. I wanted to experience a tall, bright yellow field of sunflowers? Imagine that … hmm….

Through my seasons—I've discovered to be watchful of those who will come to water the seeds for a short spell. Just as a quick "summer rain" pours down quickly… afterwards, everything is dried up in an instant. Yes, just as fast as you can blink your eye, they have disappeared, vanished … they are gone! You wonder what was their purpose, it all happened so fast? You see, my friend, God always knows exactly how much water is needed at all times! You do realize don't you that overwatering can kill some of the most beautiful blooms? Sometimes, water has to be rationed out before you begin to see one "bud" blossom into a beautiful flower.

After my heartaches–finally, I realized some come along who fertilize! You see, after all the seasons of those who had come along to sprinkle, plant, and water the seeds, full growth potential wouldn't occur without the proper fertilization. I call this the "refining season." All of our experiences up until this point was preparation for the brutal "summer heat."

You do realize in the midst of the sprinkling seeds, planting, watering and fertilization … "sun" is, an essential requirement for a beautiful, plentiful garden to flourish a harvest, right? Don't be afraid of a little heat.

If it gets too hot, just rest there for a minute. Picture yourself resting at the trunk of a tree full of life with wide, full and vibrant green leaves strong enough to block the most powerful rays of sun.

It is there my friend, where you will find relief from brutal hot temperatures. Stop dodging, stop running from pillar to post when the heat becomes too unbearable. Instead, find your place within a cool shade for a minute to cool off. Allow a rational mind to penetrate and perhaps, just perhaps you can salvage a relationship worth keeping.

Understand, just because everything is within your fingertips doesn't mean you have to reach out and grab it all, sometimes allow some things to pass you by … often times, the best is saved for last. Take your time to plant seeds, but better yet allow cultivation to enhance the beauty in your life! Watch the rain come and turn your buds into blooms.

Keep an open mind by thinking diligently, always with a positive mind. Find the *good* in people first before you point out all of the *bad* in them. We *all* are fallible. We *all* play a role in the things that occur in our lives, the course of action we take, our paths, our walks no matter how minute. You see, free will is absolutely *free*! It is given out to us all liberally. Why remain bitter, hurtful and resentful against those "you" feel wronged or hurt you in your past? Notice I said, "you" feel.

Please remember and never forget ... God allows "seasons" to pass through our lives to help *grow* us! You would not be the "seasoned cropper" you are today without those experiences. Today, rejoice, be full of life, joy and reflect God's kind of love which should exude from your pores. Smile, shine and live abundantly in peace and love!

And oh, please don't be sad for me my friend ... because I, Summer am *alive*! I passed my test and it has now become my testimony. I forgave, I learned, and now my treasures will be restored. I can now plant seeds of my own; it is a beautiful, beautiful thing!

None of us were ever perfect! Not my *daddy*, *Richard*, *Ray*, *Garrett* nor *Summer*, but through our cultivation we can now strive for perfection. You find one perfect person and it better be Jesus you are introducing me to for surely *He* is "The Most Loved!"

The Most Loved

Acknowledgements

First giving honor to God, the Head of my life, for without Him none of this would exist for me. To my parents, for leading by example: making family their priority, displaying spirituality, and emphasizing education and demonstrating strong work ethics. To my mother especially, for preaching to her children and telling us to never let anyone tell us what we could or could not do: *"Never allow your circumstances to determine your future; through Christ all things are possible."* Thank you for those inspiring words. To my father, who instilled excellence in me by taking pride in all that I do in life. And to my step-father, for removing the title "step" and becoming a second father to me, period.

To my family (siblings, aunts, uncles, and cousins) I love all of you! Many of you have touched, inspired, and influenced me so much over the years. My son, you are the reason I go on ... there are no words to describe the depth of love within my heart for you!

My close friends, near and far: Atlanta, D.C., Maryland, New York, Florida, and Arizona … you all are simply amazing. I cherish the impact each of you have had on my life–your encouragement, and your continued belief in my dreams I will never forget. Kemo, what can I say? *A Love, A Story, A Life,* all thanks to you. Lisa, my biggest cheerleader - you will always remain in my heart ... keep flying high butterfly. Quan, I asked for help–and there you were. Robin, thanks for guiding me into the realm of self-publishing. Dwayne, thanks for being my editor before I had an editor … ensuring my storyline flowed properly which ultimately pushed me into my writing frenzy. Gary, you never discouraged—always believed in me. Myrio, "fellow author" in the final moments—thanks for that extra boost to help get me to the finish line. Monica Hardwick, for announcing to the world, the birth of "The Most Loved." My photographers, videographers, audio technicians, voice over artists, graphic designers, models, interviewers: Norris Williams, Rassi Dennard, Erick Elmore, Ivan Previlon, Trevino Allen, Michael McNeil, Deneen Wright, Maggie Spicher, Kollin Brown, Leroy Watson, Rashidi Gibson, Quan Hodges, Terry Bratton, Eli Blyden, Gabriel L. Trofort, Sdot Cassanova, Bass Fungk, Angela Carter, Myrio Lemons and Mike n Me Photography —thanks for providing me all of the marketing tools necessary to market *"The Most Loved" A Love, A Story, A Life* across the globe.

So many countless others—who have been there to assist whenever I was in need of direction and/or assistance for all of my promotional efforts. I thank all of you for your continued support, for your prayers in the past and future. And last, but not least … Emily Rogers, my editor–thanks for dotting my "I's" and crossing my "T's." Emily, so happy your editing so eloquently aligned with the words I wanted to convey.

This book is also dedicated to my family and friends who are no longer here with us, but who remain in our hearts and spirits forever. I hope I make you proud!

Made in the USA
Middletown, DE
01 September 2024

60228044R00186